European Commission

CU00967589

Air pollution epidemiology reports series

Socioeconomic and cultural factors in air pollution epidemiology

Report number 8

Edited by

M. Jantunen

KTL
Ezpolis-Group
Mannerheimintie 166
Fin-003300 Helsinki

Directorate-General
Science, Research and Development

1997

EUR 17510 EN

Published by the
EUROPEAN COMMISSION

Directorate-General XII
Science, Research and Development

B-1049 Brussels

This report is a publication of the 'Environment and climate' research programme
of the European Commission, Directorate-General for Science,
Research and Development

A great deal of additional information on the European Union is available on the Internet.
It can be accessed through the Europa server (http://europa.eu.int)

Cataloguing data can be found at the end of this publication

Luxembourg: Office for Official Publications of the European Communities, 1997

ISBN 92-827-9748-1

Printed in Italy

Reports to date in the Air Pollution Epidemiology Reports Series include:

For further information on this series, please contact:

Dr. C. NOLAN
European Commission
DG XII - Directorate-General for Science, Research and Development
200, rue de la Loi
B-1049 BRUSSELS

TABLE OF CONTENTS

INTRODUCTION

Canice NOLAN

In 1990, an European Concerted Action in Air Pollution Epidemiology was established. It was initially implemented as COST project 613/2 linked to the STEP Programme, but was later run as a concerted action in the ENVIRONMENT research Programme of the Commission. The main objective of the concerted action is "to improve the quality and effectiveness of epidemiological research on atmospheric pollution and health through European cooperation".

Technical objectives of the action are:
- raising and unifying the standards of study designs, measurement techniques and data analysis methodologies (through WP-reports, peer review activities and training programmes),
- creating an European (including Central and Eastern Europe) network of experts in air pollution epidemiology (committee, working parties and workshops),
- initiating cross-European multicenter studies in air pollution epidemiology,
- identifying and addressing air pollution problems specific to some European regions (regional workshops), and
- encouraging the utilization of the unique opportunities of East-West European study comparisons, and possibilities for semi-experimental studies in Central and Eastern Europe.

No research is funded directly within the concerted action, although shared-cost action projects, which are offshoots of the action, have successfully joined the ENVIRONMENT Research Programme of the Commission.

Within the concerted action the Commission is assisted in its task of coordinating European Research by a scientific Steering Committee comprising experts appointed *ad personam* from almost all of the EEA Member States and Switzerland. Participants from WHO and from Central and Eastern European countries are also regularly invited to the meetings of the Committee.

Working groups are established by the Commission on the advice of the Steering Committee to implement specific tasks. These groups meet regularly at workshops etc. to produce Air Pollution Epidemiology Research Reports. To date, three working groups have produced reports on: (i) Exposure Assessment, (ii) Health Effects Assessment, and (iii) Study Designs. One more working group is currently preparing a report on (iv) Risk Assessment. This report should be ready in 1997.

The first ECA Air Pollution Epidemiology workshop report dealt with Time-Activity Patterns. The present Air Pollution Epidemiology Report emanates from a Workshop on Socioeconomic and Cultural Factors in air pollution epidemiology. This European Commission research workshop was hosted by the EC/DG XII in Brussels in March, 1995. This report addresses the various confounding and modifying impacts that social, economic, ethnic and cultural factors may have on the time-activity patterns, levels of air pollution exposures, health status, and questionnaire responses of different groups in a community. It also discusses the techniques by which socioeconomic and cultural factors can be measured and incorporated into study designs in air pollution epidemiology.

In addition, regional aspects of air pollution are treated in special scientific symposia. To date, three sets of proceedings have been produced following (i) an East European / COST Meeting in Air Pollution Epidemiology (Budapest, May 1991), (ii) a Workshop on Air Pollution and Health in the Mediterranean Region of Europe (Athens, October 1992), and a Workshop on Air Pollution Epidemiology - Experiences in Eastern and Western Europe (Berlin, November, 1994).

General Overview of the Significance of Socio-economic Factors on Health in Europe

Anton E. Kunst

Department of Public Health, Erasmus University POBox 1738, 3000 DR Rotterdam, The Netherlands

INTRODUCTION

The purposes of this paper are

- to describe the associations between health and socio-economic factors by means of illustrations from various parts of Europe (section 2);

- to provide an explanatory scheme that helps us to better understand these associations (section 3);

- to discuss the relevance of socio-economic factors to air pollution epidemiology and the relevance of air pollution to social epidemiology (section 4).

SOCIO-ECONOMIC FACTORS AND HEALTH: SIX ILLUSTRATIONS

Each illustration in this section stresses a different aspect of the association between socio-economic factors and health in Europe. For more extensive documentation we refer to a number of overviews (1-3).

1. The association between health and socio-economic factors is observed in each European country for which data are available.

Figure 1 shows for different countries from the northern, western and southern part of Europe that less education is associated with higher risk of dying prematurely. Smaller differences are found in countries like Sweden and the Netherlands, but these inequalities are far from being eliminated. Higher mortality rates among lower socio-economic groups are also observed for some central and eastern European countries such as Hungary and Bulgaria (2). The persistent nature of socio-economic inequalities in health also became manifest in trend studies which found that these inequalities have not diminished over time but, at least with respect to mortality, even widened (4)

2. The association between socio-economic factors and health is often very strong

Table 1 shows social class differences in mortality by some causes of death in France. Mortality differences are particularly large for liver cirrhosis, respiratory diseases and cancers of the upper digestive tract, with the mortality rates of semi-skilled labourers more than 3 times the rates of higher-level employees. Differences of this magnitude are not uncommon in Europe. Large differences are

3

observed in particular for men at middle age (say, 30-55 years) and for mortality from respiratory and gastro-intestinal diseases.

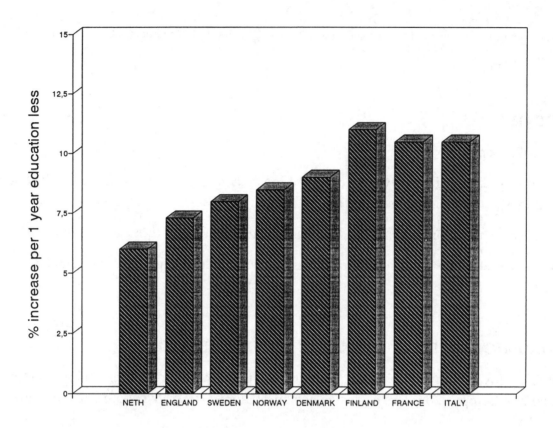

Figure 1.   The association between mortality and level of education (expressed as numbers of years of education) in 8 European countries. Men, circa 1970-1980, 35-54 years. Source: Kunst and Mackenbach (5) unpublished data.

Table 1.   Mortality ratio of semi-skilled labourers versus higher-level employees and professionals. France, 1976-1980, men 55-64 years. Source: Desplanques (6).

Cause of death	Ratio	Cause of death	Ratio
Neoplasms	1.85	Cancer of lung	1.74
Circulatory diseases	1.37	Cancer of upper digestive tract	5.23
Respiratory diseases	3.45	Cancer of stomach	2.93
Liver cirrhosis	4.68	Cancer of colon	1.30
All causes	1.84	Other neoplasms	1.22

3. Socio-economic factors are related to a broad spectrum of health problems

The previous illustration referred to mortality by cause of death. Figure 2 illustrates that socio-economic factors are also related to other aspects of diseases, in this case to their prevalence. Lower social classes in the city of Amsterdam suffer more often from a wide range of diseases, including respiratory and cardiovascular diseases. Health interview survey data from various countries consistently demonstrate large socio-economic inequalities in the prevalence of various diseases and in the prevalence of their consequences, such as physical complaints and disability (7). Inequalities in the incidence of disease have been demonstrated by epidemiological studies (e.g. on heart disease) and disease registers (e.g. cancer registers).

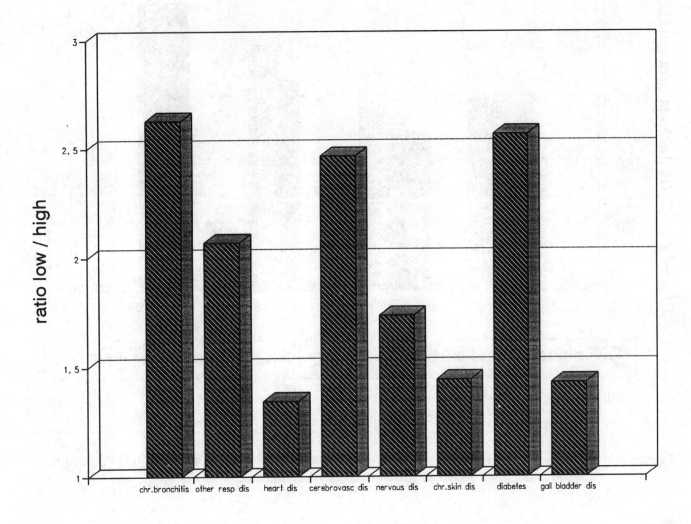

Figure 2. **Ratio of disease prevalence in unskilled labourers versus higher-level employees and professionals. Amsterdam, 1984, men and women 55-79 year. Source: van den Bos (8).**

4. Several socio-economic factors are independently related to health

Health is associated with a wide range of socio-economic indicators, including educational level, occupational class, income level and material standards of living. Each of these indicators seems to make an independent contribution to variation in health within the population. This point is illustrated in figure 3 with data from Finland: mortality is related to the people's occupation irrespectively of their education, and vice versa.

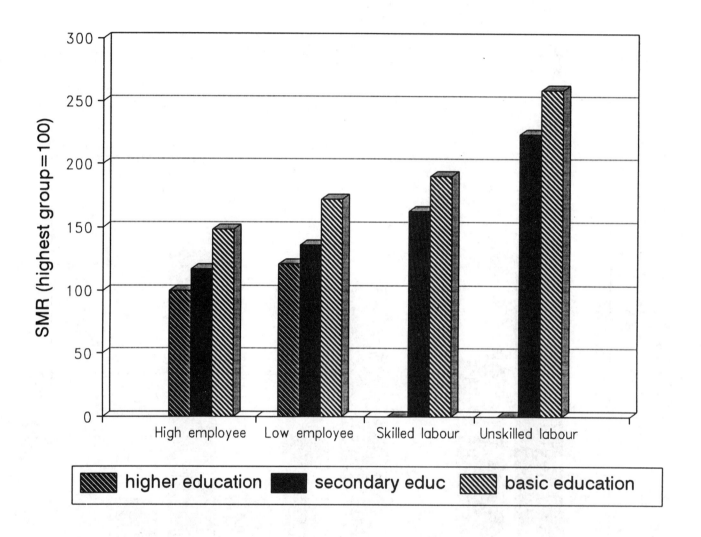

Figure 3.   **Age-standardised mortality by occupational class and educational level. Finland, 1971-1985, men 35-64 years. Source: Valkonen *et al.* (9).**

5. Health and socio-economic factors are related throughout the social ladder

Figure 4 shows the association between income and poor general health in Spain. It exemplifies a pattern of association that is observed in various countries: the association between income and health is observed both at the lower and the upper part of the income hierarchy; there is no clear threshold effect.

This also applies to other socio-economic factors. For example, in each country for which data are available, education and health are related across the entire educational hierarchy (5,7).

6. The association between socio-economic factors and health re-appears among areas

Since the socio-economic composition of areas differ, it is no surprise that health differences between areas can in part be attributed to socio-economic factors. This association has been demonstrated in many cities. For example, the life expectancy of people living in better-off districts in Budapest is about 4 years higher than that of people living in deprived districts (figure 5). Mortality differences of a similar order of magnitude are found among larger areas such as provinces or regions (11).

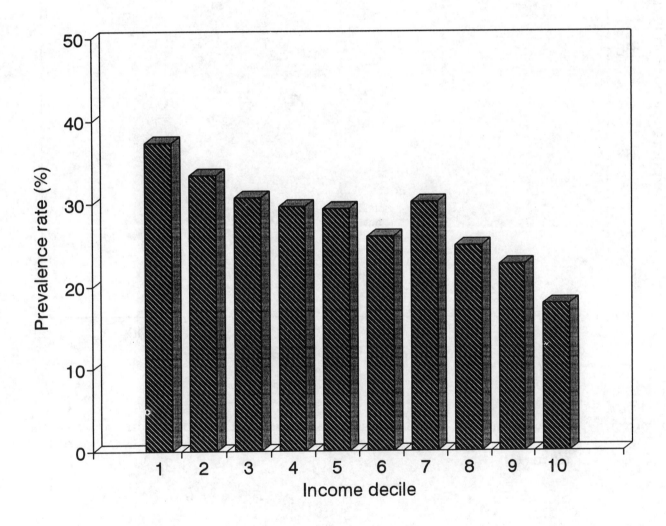

Figure 4. Prevalence of self-reported 'less-than-good' general health by income decile. Spain, 1987, men 20-74 years. Source: the National Health Interview Survey (10), unpublished data.

The results of some studies suggest that the association between area-based deprivation and health is to some extent independent of other socio-economic factors such as the residents' individual occupation (12). This suggests that living in a socio-economically disadvantaged area is in itself associated with poorer health.

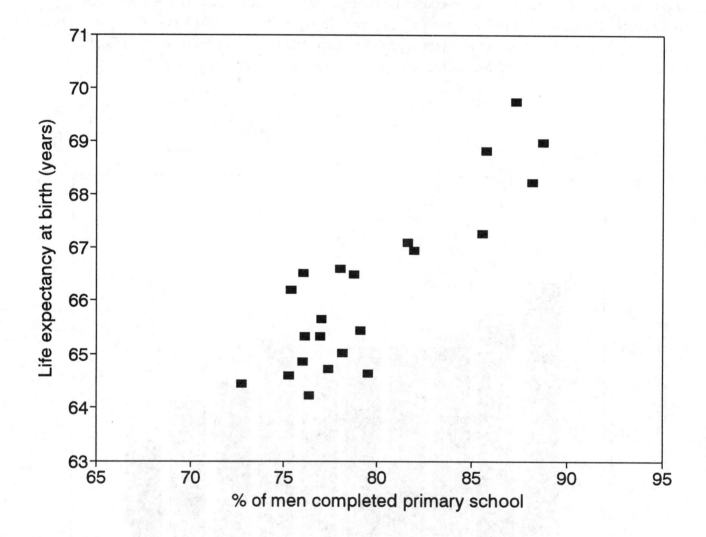

Figure 5. **Life expectancy at birth in the districts of Budapest according to percentage of men in these districts who have completed primary school. Men, 1980-1983. Source: Józan (13)**

UNDERSTANDING THE ASSOCIATION BETWEEN SOCIO-ECONOMIC FACTORS AND HEALTH

The association between health and socio-economic factors is extremely complex (14). The scheme presented below, which is adopted from Mackenbach (15) represents the many ties that can link health and socio-economic factors. This scheme is not complete because it ignores, for example, the role of living conditions in childhood. Still, however, it is sufficiently developed to clarify the 5 issues that we would like to stress.

Position in social stratification system (SES)	Implications of that position for the people's personal life	Prevalence of risk factors for disease incidence and prognosis	Disease process
Education	Knowledge, skills, access to information Attitudes, values, tastes, social norms	Behavioral factors - physical exercise - smoking - dietary habits - alcohol consumption	Incidence
Occupation	Power, prestige, place in social networks Daily activities and tasks, unemployment Insurance for medical care, unemployment and old age	Psycho-social factors - experience of stress - social support - coping styles Use and quality of care - preventive care - other medical care	Outcome - death - prevalence - symptoms - disability Prognosis
Income	Access to scarce material goods and services	Environmental exposures - at work - at home - during transport	

| ===> | ===> | ===> | Causation |
| <-- | | | Selection |

1. Socio-economic status and its 3 core indicators

People are unequal. Some have a more advantaged position in society than others. These differences between people can be usually portrayed as a social stratification system. People occupy a position in that system according to their (partner's) job, their educational achievement, and their income level or standard of living. These three socio-economic factors are generally regarded as the core indicators of the people's position in the social stratification system. That position is usually referred to as *socioeconomic status* (SES). The term *social class* could be applied when occupation is used as the core indicator; it refers to groups of people with a similar position in the labour market.

2. Two mechanisms: causation and selection

Socio-economic status and health are related in basically two ways.

a. The causation mechanism: the socio-economic status of people influences their health. Our scheme illustrates that the personal life of people is influenced by the position they have in society, and that differences in life spheres imply differences in the prevalence of specific risk factors for disease.

b. The selection mechanism: the possibility that persons attain and maintain a certain position in society is influenced by their health and by factors closely related to health such as the readiness to invest in future.

The reality is more complex than this distinction suggests. For example, a child that suffers from asthma or *diabetes mellitus* may have problems to complete a high education and achieve a good job (the selection mechanism) whereas the resulting low SES may in later life aggravate the pre-existing disease (the causation mechanism). In cases like this, an intricate association between health and socioeconomic factors is formed over the individual's life course.

3. The causation mechanism: a great diversity of pathways

Many routes lead from low socio-economic status to bad health. A simple causal pathway seems to be that the higher lung cancer mortality of lower class people is explained by their higher tobacco consumption. But even in this case the explanation is more complex than it seems. Other risk factors for lung cancer such as exposure to toxic compounds in ambient air may make an additional contribution or act synergistically with smoking. In addition, the question remains *why* people in lower classes smoke more: due to failure to recognise the health hazards of smoking, as a way of coping with their higher levels of daily stress, and/or due to attitudes and social norms that are more conducive to smoking?

4. The generalised character of socio-economic inequalities in health

The great diversity of the ties that link socio-economic status and health may help us to understand why inequalities in health persist over time and are still found in all European societies; why a wide array of diseases is involved; why both education, occupation and income make independent contributions; and why inequalities in health are not confined to the lower part of the social hierarchy. For example, the fact that inequalities in health in Sweden are still substantial (5,7), despite its highly developed social security system and small income inequalities, is not so surprising when it is realised that not all ties that link socio-economic status and health need to involve the material factors that are given in the lower left corner of our scheme.

5. The place of air pollution

In the scheme, air pollution is one of the risk factors that is casually in between socioeconomic status and disease. For example, high levels of air pollution may contribute to the higher morbidity and mortality rates that are usually found among residents of deprived urban districts. Important to note is that in cases like this, air pollution does not come alone. Inhabitants of poor and polluted districts are likely to be more often exposed to several other risk factors for disease, including substandard housin and less healthy life styles. In addition, these risk factors may act synergistically with air pollution in causing death and disease.

SOCIO-ECONOMIC FACTORS, AIR POLLUTION AND HEALTH: THREE AREAS OF CONCERN

1. Socio-economic factors as confounders in air pollution epidemiology

Observational studies in air pollution epidemiology can grossly be divided in two types: time series analysis on a single population, and comparative analysis of exposed populations and less exposed populations. If, in the latter type of study, socio-economic factors are unequally distributed among exposed and less exposed individuals, the researcher faces the problem of confounding. This is difficult problem to cope with because of the strong and diverse ties that link socio-economic factors to health. Essential is an accurate measurement of education, occupation and income, either for the demarcation of case and control groups, or for control in later statistical analyses.

Note from the scheme presented above that a low education, occupation or income does not directly cause ill-health, but that its effect on health is mediated by specific risk factors for disease. Control for socioeconomic factors would therefore be superfluous if control could be made for the most important risk factors by which socieconomic factors exert an effect on health. Tobacco consumption is an example of a risk factor that most studies on air pollution epidemiology control for. But it is not the only relevant risk factor. Several other risk factors are likely to be linked to socioeconomic factors, but many of them are not controlled for. Some risk factors re difficult to measure adequately (e.g. psychosocial stress); some other factors may not even yet have been identified as risk factors for disease. Control for socioeconomic factors themselves are then a way to control for the confounding that is inherent to air pollution studies than compare populations with different SES.

2. Air pollution as an explanatory variable in social epidemiology

Increased exposure to air pollution is one of the many factors that might contribute to the poorer health of lower socio-economic groups, such as those living in deprived urban districts. This raises a few still unanswered questions to social epidemiology: to what extent are lower socio-economic groups more exposed to specific pollutants? does this increased exposure make a substantial contribution to the increased prevalence of respiratory and other diseases among lower socio-economic groups?

3. Effect modification: an area of mutual concern

It is likely that lower socio-economic groups not only are exposed to higher levels of air pollution, but in addition have an increased risk of developing symptoms and disease when exposed to a certain level of air pollution. Increased susceptibility can occur because of a higher prevalence of, among others, tobacco consumption, pre-existing disease (e.g. asthma), impaired defense systems, exposure to multiple environmental hazards (at work, home and traffic), and inadequate use of health care (16).

One implication is that in the analysis of the health effects of air pollution the statistical control for socio-economic factors should include effect modification parameters. In addition, the restriction of the analysis to lower socio-economic groups may help the researcher to detect air pollution effects which otherwise cannot be discerned.

The possibility that lower socio-economic groups are not only more exposed but also more susceptible to air pollution is an extra reason to assess the contribution of air pollution to the poorer health of these groups. After all, there are a few reasons for their poorer health that can be considered so 'unfair' (17) as being more susceptible to and at the same time more exposed to air pollution.

REFERENCES

1. Mielck A, Rosario Giraldez M (eds). Inequalities in health and health care. Review of selected publications from 18 Western European Countries. Waxmann, Münster/New York, 1993.
2. Illsley R, Svensson P-G (eds). Social inequalities in health. *Social Science and Medicine* 1990; **31** (special issue): 223-240.
3. Fox J (ed). Health inequalities in European countries, Gower, Aldershot (UK), 1989.
4. Kunst AE, Mackenbach JP. Measuring socio-economic inequalities in health. World Health Organization, Copenhagen, 1994.
5. Kunst AE, Mackenbach JP. The size of mortality differences associated with educational level in nine industrialized countries. *American Journal of Public Health* 1994; **84**: 932-937.
6. Desplanques G. La mortalité des adults: Résultats de 2 etudes longitudinales (période 1955-1980). INSEE, Paris, 1984.
7. Kunst AE, Geurts JJM, van den Berg J. International variation of socio-economic inequalities in self-reported health. *Journal of Epidemiology and Community Health* 1995; **49**; 117-123.
8. Bos GAM. van den. Zorgen van en voor chronisch zieken [Care for the chronically ill]. Bohn, Scheltema & Holkema, Amsterdam, 1989.
9. Valkonen T, Martelin T, Rimpelä A. Socio-economic mortality differences in Finland 1971-85. Statistics Finland, Helsinki, 1990.
10. Encuesta Nacional de Salud [National Health Interview Survey]. Ministry of Health and Consumer Affairs, Madrid, 1989.
11. Decroly JM, Vanlaer J, Grimmeau JP et al. Atlas de la population européenne, Editions de l'Université de Bruxelles, Bruxelles, 1991.
12. Townsend P, Phillimore P, Beattie A. Health and deprivation. Inequality in the North. Croom Helm, London, 1988.
13. Józan P. An ecological study of mortality differentials in Budapest 1980-1983. Part I. Central Statistical Office, Budapest, 1987.
14. Davey Smith G, Blane D, Bartley M. Explanations for socio-economic differentials in mortality: evidence from Britain and elsewhere. *Eur J Public Health* 1994; **4**: 131-144.
15. Mackenbach JP. Social inequalities and health differences: an overview of the findings from the literature (in Dutch). In: Wetenschappelijke Raad Rederingsbeleid. "The unequal distribution of health. The Hague: Staatsuitgeverij, 1987.
16. Sexton K, Gong H, Bailar JC et al. Air pollution health risks: do class and race matter? *Toxicol and Indust Health* 1993; **9**: 843-878.
17. Whitehead M. The concepts and principles of equity and health. World Health Organization, Copenhagen, 1990.

THE LIMITATIONS OF SOCIOECONOMIC INDICATORS: A CULTURAL PERSPECTIVE ON THE RECOGNITION OF SOCIAL DIVERSITY IN AIR POLLUTION EPIDEMIOLOGY

Peter Phillimore

Department of Social Policy, University of Newcastle, Newcastle Upon Tyne NE1 7RU, U.K.

SUMMARY

In what ways are social and cultural factors important in air pollution epidemiology? How should air pollution epidemiology take into account the culture of peoples exposed to pollution? This paper will discuss these two questions, drawing on two studies of the health effects of industrial air pollution in northeast England. They reflect the growing recognition that epidemiological studies require the contribution of several disciplines; and that the more straightforward measurements of social and economic status (whether of individuals or households) can only be a first step towards an understanding of social and cultural variations between groups. However, from the point of view of a sociologist or social anthropologist, there are definite limits to the extent to which social and cultural variations between groups can adequately be encompassed in epidemiological studies. Given the likelihood that there will be an increasing number of air pollution studies in future, this paper will consider both the benefits and difficulties associated with the use of social and cultural data.

INTRODUCTION

What social and cultural factors are sufficiently important that they should be considered in studies of the health effects of air pollution? The tendency in the past has been to rely on a limited set of indicators of socioeconomic status, these being seen as surrogates for wider differences in social and cultural experience. A great deal is lost, however, by such reductionism, even if it may be the only option available. This paper considers some further ways in which social and cultural factors are relevant in air pollution epidemiology.

The themes discussed in this paper derive from two recent studies in northeast England. These have examined the impact of air pollution from industrial operations on the health of residents living nearby. The first was a study of the last coking works on the River Tyne, which closed in 1990 (1,2,3). The second compared larger populations: Sunderland and Teesside. Teesside has a concentration of petrochemical and steel production close to major residential areas that is unmatched in Britain, and has been an area where there has been public concern for many years about the health consequences of air pollution, fuelled in part by evidence of extremely high mortality in many localities (4; also Moffatt *et al.* in this volume; for earlier work on Teesside and Sunderland, see 5,6). In both studies, the importance of the social went beyond the traditional (and necessary) attempt to devise adequate operational measures of socioeconomic status.

I would argue that social and cultural factors may be particularly important in three main ways in air pollution studies.

i.   The identification and selection of populations with similar characteristics.
ii.   People's experience of and response to potential or actual exposure to air pollution.
iii.   People's experience of and response to ill-health that they themselves perceive to be attributable to exposure to pollution.

The first of these is the context in which air pollution studies readily acknowledge the importance of socioeconomic or cultural factors in the design or analysis stages of research; the latter two relate more to interpretation than design, but are too often represented by non-social scientists as personal or individual matters, overlooking their social and cultural significance. This paper will discuss these in turn. In each context there are characteristic problems in handling sociocultural factors, and the intention here is not to suggest a set of procedures which solve these problems. The more limited aim is to highlight certain characteristic difficulties faced in the epidemiology of air pollution.

Particular attention will be paid to cultural characteristics and influences. Distinctions between what is social and what is cultural are not hard and fast, particularly in a transnational context where different histories have influenced usage. But it will suffice here to suggest a distinction between evidence that relates to the structure of society, particularly the characteristics of social inequality; and evidence which relates to the ways people live, the pattern of their lives, and the values which underlie such patterns of living. I take culture to refer to the latter. People's perceptions and understandings of their life experiences are thus critical for an appreciation of culture.

DEFINING THE SOCIAL AND CULTURAL CHARACTERISTICS OF STUDIED POPULATIONS

If socioeconomic and cultural factors are powerful determinants of health, as has long been established, how do epidemiological studies of the potential impact of air pollution take into account the independent effects of these socioeconomic and cultural influences upon the health of populations under study? Furthermore, are these effects wholly independent of the effects of air pollution? These questions arise because, in all but catastrophic circumstances, the impact of air pollution on human health is likely to be overshadowed by factors other than pollution. They draw attention to the confounding or effect modifying role of social and cultural influences. In consequence, studies are designed to match populations as closely as possible, to ensure the comparison of like with like. Alternatively adjustment for social differences will be undertaken during statistical analysis. Sometimes an approach is adopted combining both procedures.

Yet how far is it necessary to go to match study populations? The problem may be highlighted by describing the steps that can be taken to ensure that the socioeconomic characteristics of the population are adequately reflected. As a first step, the most common procedure in Britain over the last decade has been to use the national census to classify geographical areas - down to the level of the 100 metre grid square or an area (the enumeration district) containing approximately 150 households. The social characteristics of geographical entities may then be defined through indicators such as unemployment rates. Further sub-classification is possible. For instance, youth unemployment rates may be singled out; or unemployment among those aged over 55 years, a category of those who are unlikely to be employed again (7). The versatility of such area-based indicators should not be underestimated. Nevertheless, there are inevitably many aspects of life and living conditions not covered by a census.

Even so, the problems in this context are not huge, and tend to concern a lack of precision or specificity in the available data, whether these come from a national census or special surveys. There has been periodic debate in Britain about how well variations in car ownership reflect variations in disposable income, or how well housing tenure reflects wealth in the sense of overall assets given different regional traditions (8). The census indicators used for comparing the characteristics of small areas in the two studies in northeast England are shown in Table 1.

Table 1.   **Census indicators examined in two studies in north-east England**

Main indicators
% Households with no car
% Unemployed men and women
% Unemployed 16-24 year old individuals
% Single parent households
% Lone pensioners
% Renting home
% Residents in overcrowded households
% 17 year old individuals in full-time education

Supporting indicators
% Male unemployed
% Female unemployed
% Children in single parent families
% Moving house within previous 12 months
% Living in Local Authority rented home
% Households with shared bathroom and toilet
% Households with no children
% Head of household born in 'new Commonwealth'/Pakistan

Of course additional information can be sought in specially tailored social surveys. As a second step in both the studies in northeast England mentioned above, postal surveys were conducted using a random sample of the populations of interest. The intention here was partly to collect individual data that matched the census data, as a check to ensure that the selected sample reflected the socioeconomic characteristics of the area in which they lived, to take into account the problem of the so-called `ecological fallacy'. But it was equally important to try to supplement the census data, to fill in gaps in the social picture of the population under consideration. Details about smoking habits or alcohol consumption, or dietary preferences, could thus be accommodated in the overall picture alongside details about length of residence, housing conditions or occupational history. In each case, the potential of such factors to have a bearing on any assessment of the impact of localised air pollution is considerable. Examples of social and cultural data sought in these surveys are given in Table 2 below.

In this context, is there anything important which is beyond the reach of such supplementary surveys? For a social scientist, perhaps the main gaps have to do with the consequences of different kinds of *social relationship*. Here we move more clearly to the cultural sphere, for mapping relationships is unlikely to tell you much about how they are experienced. Different kinds of social ties - and the support these provide - can only be captured crudely in a survey. This is important, because when we describe an area as a neighbourhood we are inclined to make assumptions about people relating to one another, often speculating on the extent to which those who live in a particular area rely on or support one another, and the extent to which this may be based on ties of kinship or not. Two neighbourhoods may have very similar socioeconomic characteristics, but radically different cultural ambiences, a distinction that may well have a bearing on health patterns. I would hesitate to decry all attempts to capture this dimension of culture through a survey - we have attempted such an exercise in our present work (see Table 2). But it would be self-deluding to pretend that it is anything but a highly reductionist approach to the cultural.

Table 2.   Examples of social indicators not available from national census

Housing
How many years lived at current address
How many years lived in same neighbourhood
Housing conditions (damp, mould)
Heating and cooking sources of energy

Work
Main occupations at different stages of working life
Duration of working life in a range of industries of interest
Frequency of exposure to dust, fumes or chemicals, extremes of temperature

Local services
Accessibility of family doctor
Mode of transport to family doctor

Social support & morale
Sources of social support in times of difficulty
Causes of worry and stress

Health-related consumption
Smoking history
Alcohol consumption
Fresh fruit and vegetable consumption
Physical exercise in leisure time

A parallel concern may be identified in relation to occupational experience. This may be illustrated by reference to an earlier discussion on the divergent mortality observed in Teesside and Sunderland. Through most of the 20th Century, until the economic contraction of the 1980s, the main industries of Sunderland were coal-mining and shipbuilding; the main industries of Teesside steel and petrochemicals. All are occupations posing widely recognised risks for those employed. Less tangible are differences in working practices. In an earlier publication I raised the possibility that shipbuilding and coal-mining both gave more scope to craft skill, individual judgement and small team autonomy in work than steel and chemical plant employment, and that this might be a factor affecting the more intangible issues of morale and well-being at work (6). I would not wish to make too much of this, but it calls attention to aspects of the experience of occupations which are too easily overlooked in simple occupational classifications.

Part of the difficulty is that it has always been easier to devise operational definitions of socioeconomic status than of cultural characteristics. Even though there is a large sociological literature on the

16

conceptual problems of measuring social class, for example, individuals can be placed in categories on the basis of occupation, education, income, or type of housing. The classifications generated out of such data provide a guide to gradations of inequality. With slightly greater difficulty household versions of such classifications can also be created. But cultural characteristics are less amenable to measurement, and consequently are less easily accommodated in research designs built around quantitative analyses. Two tendencies have been apparent. The first has been to reduce culture to lifestyle, and then to reduce lifestyle to health-related behaviour. In this way, smoking, alcohol consumption, and some indicators of food consumption and physical exertion have become ways of measuring cultural characteristics. The second has been to classify individuals by an ethnic label, an issue to which I now turn.

In the same way that studies may control for social class, a common approach has been to control in analyses for ethnicity or nationality. But this begs the question: for what are we controlling? Is it to do with assumptions about standard of living, or style of living - in which case why not turn to indicators which reflect these more directly? Or is it an acknowledgement of identity? This in turn would beg another question: what is it about a person's ethnicity or cultural identity that the study sees it as important to reflect? While sensitivity to cultural diversity is a prerequisite for comparison - in this field as in any other - it is not obvious that the objective is advanced by controlling for ethnicity on the basis of labels assigned either at a census or through a survey. For the procedures used in these sources ignore sharp socioeconomic differences within groups and - a more serious shortcoming - objectify and misconstrue the fluidity of identity (and labels of identity) in today's world.

The essential point is that there are limits to what can be achieved with socioeconomic indicators - from official or specifically tailored sources. Such data cannot describe what life is like and what it means to live in one neighbourhood or one city rather than another. This is to anticipate the discussion in the following section.

One final point should be made in this section about attempts to eliminate potential social or cultural confounders. What are seen as *confounding* factors in an epidemiological framework, may well be seen as *compounding* factors in a sociological one. Important though the concept of confounding is for measurement within epidemiology, it has the drawback that it tends to be operationalised as if causal influences are separate and distinct. But it is important also to recognise the interactive, mutually reinforcing effects of various influences upon health. Just as pollutants may interact, creating effects that are more than additive, so sociologists would argue that the social must not be reduced to separate, discrete ingredients, with individual effects that are interpreted along dose-response lines. Damp housing, low income, harsh working conditions, and stresses associated with poor services or crime or unemployment, are likely to have a cumulative impact on health. Influences such as these may in turn accentuate the health impact of air pollution in a way that the language of `confounding' too readily overlooks (2,3).

THE EXPERIENCE OF AIR POLLUTION AND ILL-HEALTH: A SOCIAL SCIENTIFIC APPROACH TO THE CULTURAL

The second problem is one aspect of the reality facing all air pollution epidemiology - that measurement is being attempted in circumstances far removed from the laboratory setting implicit in case-control methodology. Social life defies the order represented by laboratory-derived methods. The social-cultural world intrudes on, or interferes with, measurement in various ways. This can be illustrated by reference to the studies previously mentioned in northeast England. At a practical level, as we have discovered in Teesside, all attempts to plot localised variations in pollution across a city are continually thwarted by vandalism. 'Safe' sites for air quality monitoring seem hard to find. In a city where we were told by a medical officer in one industrial company, "I think you'll find people are more concerned about crime than about pollution", the very task of measuring pollution is itself vulnerable to the same disaffection and alienation that gives rise to crime.

If one source of potential ambiguity comes from the problems of actually measuring air quality across a city, another source comes from the way that the population are regarded as being themselves `contaminated' by over one hundred years of debates about air pollution on Teesside. The fact that illness is not just a biological or physiological matter but is also expressed, recognised and responded to in ways which reflect the cultural conventions of a particular setting, has always posed a problem for a measurement-based science like epidemiology, which finds it hard to avoid treating the social construction of illness as other than a variety of artefact - `noise' in the data that needs screening out. The concept of `awareness bias' is the outcome of this methodological concern. Clarity in `case definition' has always been central to epidemiology. Yet the further away from the clinical setting and biomedical procedures that research on public health moves, the more elusive a notion case definition can become. The measurement of ill-health is easily seen in epidemiology as compromised by the preoccupations of the population under scrutiny (either about forms of illness or sources of health risk). In the last analysis, this leads to the discarding of data as simply unreliable - any biological bedrock being too `contaminated' by cultural or psychosocial overlay to be accessible (i.e. measurable). This is an understandable response. Recognition of this cultural overlay sits uneasily with comparison of like-with-like, on which epidemiological measurement necessarily rests. This approach and these difficulties are of course by no means confined to those who describe themselves as epidemiologists. They govern the procedures all of us adopt when we are seeking to reach conclusions about patterns of health in the population. The way that is sought out of the impasse generally involves a call for better (more sensitive or diverse) indicators and better techniques of measurement - yet that sidesteps rather than faces the issues involved, because it rests on the misguided assumption that a bedrock of `real' ill-health can somehow be distilled, if only our techniques were up to it (2).

The dilemma may be illustrated through the quotation below. Responding to the findings of the Monkton Coking Works study, on Tyneside (1), that patterns of acute respiratory ill-health were consistently related to short-term pollution from coking operations, a sympathetic reviewer in The Lancet wrote:

> "The conclusions seem plausible and the researchers and residents may have arrived at the correct conclusion regarding health hazards...[But] overall, the arguments for refuting awareness bias are not entirely convincing" (9).

There can be no entirely satisfactory resolution of this problem, and Malmberg's remarks provide an acknowledgement of the dilemma. But for sociologists or social anthropologists a major difficulty with the epidemiological paradigm is that it tends to discount or underplay the experiences of those who are being studied (see 2,3). If people's awareness of an issue poses problems for measurement and interpretation, so equally would our subjects being unaware: from a sociological perspective the fact that our subjects of study have prior awareness of the topics we investigate is a precondition for our knowledge as researchers.

In the postal questionnaires used in the two studies in northeast England, respondents were invited to add

18

any further remarks they wished to make. Around the Monkton Coking Works, many replies dwelt upon the improvement to personal respiratory health or the health of those they knew that was anticipated from the closure of the site. In the context of Teesside, a different emphasis was apparent, as many respondents tried to weigh up the trade-off between industrial pollution and industrial employment. Two examples are typical:

> "I feel it would be nice to live in a cleaner environment, but I feel the loss of jobs would cause more health problems" (33 years old Teesside woman).

> "Common sense tells you that a cleaner environment is essential, but for jobs to be lost would also affect people's health. So which is the greater evil? I just honestly don't know" (mother of two children, Teesside).

Social scientists have generally argued that public concerns or preoccupations are themselves data - not barriers to data. Such views are of interest as they may enhance interpretation rather than distort the `facts of the matter'. This is achieved through providing a context within which to interpret evidence, the rationale being that understanding of context is crucial to interpretation. Although writing about land-based toxic waste and its impact on a local population, Brown's general argument is relevant:

> "Many people who live at risk of toxic hazards have access to data otherwise inaccessible to scientists. Their experiential knowledge usually precedes official and scientific awareness, largely because it is so tangible. Knowledge of toxic hazards in communities and workplaces in the last two decades has often stemmed from lay observation" (10).

A figure in a dispute involving contamination in Pittsfield (USA) echoes the same theme:

> "This is the area we grew up in and we know the problem, better than management. They've only been here a short period of time. I'm sure they meant no harm; they've been cooperative, but none-the-less, we have the problem" (11).

Issues like these illuminate problems of method in air pollution epidemiology. But the themes discussed in this section also reflect a social scientist's perspective on how greater recognition can be accorded to the cultural. Giving greater recognition to the cultural dimension of life in air pollution epidemiology is not just about characterising groups or sub-groups in more subtle ways. More importantly, it is about rethinking whether we can incorporate elements of how people experience their lives. The concept of awareness bias has been discussed because - for all its utility - it is one of the devices in epidemiology that places in jeopardy a fuller, more rounded recognition of the place of culture.

CONCLUDING COMMENTS

Epidemiological studies have sought to incorporate social or cultural factors in study design by assuming that individual or household or neighbourhood *characteristics* can stand as surrogates for social *experience*. There are good grounds for this approach, in the sense that it is possible to operationalise measures of characteristics, but not of social experience. Nevertheless, this paper has sought to draw attention to some of the ways in which cultural experience is not reducible to social characteristics, but may still be extremely relevant in studies of the health effects of air pollution. Since this is the case within one small part of Britain, how much more this applies when cross-national comparisons are undertaken. In the field of air pollution epidemiology, the cultural dimension is relevant in the understanding and assumptions about pollution that prevail among those being studied, and in the ways that people respond to ill-health. The field of sickness behaviour is of course the ground on which epidemiologists and health sociologists meet. There are no neat solutions to the difficulties highlighted in this paper. The central dilemma in studying patterns of illness or morbidity is how to combine fidelity to individual or collective experience with comparability. The one effectively precludes the other. For fidelity means framing within a particular cultural context - yet that is to rule out comparison. While making comparison the objective inevitably means masking cultural differences. Yet in the last analysis there could be much greater recognition of the part played by cultural factors in air pollution epidemiology. That, coupled with a more sensitive approach to analysis which does not attempt to iron out these factors, may indeed assist interpretation of what will continue to be complex, multifaceted studies.

ACKNOWLEDGEMENTS

This paper has been written in conjunction with Dr Suzanne Moffatt, and reflects ideas developed jointly in many discussions.

REFERENCES

1. Bhopal R, Phillimore P, Moffatt S, Foy C. Is living near a coking works harmful to health? A study of industrial air pollution. *Journal Epidemiology and Community Health*. 1994; 48: 237-247.
2. Phillimore P, Moffatt S. Discounted knowledge: Local experience, environmental pollution and health. In Popay J and Williams G. *Researching the people's health*. Routledge, London, 1994, pp 134-156.
3. Moffatt S. Phillimore P, Bhopal R, Foy C. "If this is what it's doing to our washing, what is it doing to our lungs?" Industrial pollution and public understanding in North-East England. *Social Science and Medicine* 1995; 41: 883-891.
4. Teesside Environmental Epidemiology Study (TEES) Group. Health, illness and the environment in Teesside and Sunderland. A Report. Newcastle University, 1995.
5. Phillimore P, Morris D. Discrepant legacies: premature mortality in two industrial towns. *Social Science and Medicine* 1991; 33: 139-152.
6. Phillimore P. How do places shape health? Rethinking locality and lifestyle in north-east England. In, Platt, S et.al. *Locating Health: Sociological and Historical Explorations*. Avebury, Aldershot, 1993, pp 163-177.
7. Gordon et al 1995 People and places 2: social and economic distinctions in England. Bristol University: SAUS Publications.
8. Townsend P, Phillimore P, Beattie A. *Health and Deprivation. Inequality and the North*. Croom Helm, London, 1988.
9. Malmberg P. Coking to death? *Lancet* 1994; 344: 632.
10. Brown P. Popular epidemiology and toxic waste contamination: lay and professional ways of knowing. *Journal of Health and Social Behaviour* 1992; 33: 267-281.
11. Nash J, Kirsch M. Polychlorinated biphenyls in the electrical machinery industry: an ethnological study of community action and corporate responsibility. *Social Science and Medicine*, 1986; 23,2: 131-138.

APPLICATION OF SOCIOECONOMIC FACTORS IN AIR POLLUTION EPIDEMIOLOGY STUDIES

Norbert Englert

Institute for Water, Soil and Air Hygiene of the Federal Environmental Agency
Corrensplatz 1, D-14195 Berlin, Germany

SUMMARY

In all types of air pollution epidemiology studies, socioeconomic factors have to be adequately included because they may lead to misclassification of exposure and effects as well as interactions. This is a well-known problem in cross-sectional and case control studies, but it can also influence the slope of a dose-response relationship found in time-series studies.

INTRODUCTION

To include socioeconomic factors in the analysis of relations between air pollution and health effects is a necessity that nowadays is generally accepted as a theoretical prerequisite. But very often one can hear the opinion that confounding by socioeconomic factors is only a problem in cross-sectional studies, whereas time series studies are not affected because participating individuals act as their own controls.

This explanation, as all simple explanations do, runs the risk of neglecting important aspects. Figure 1 shows the major points where socioeconomic factors can influence exposure-effect relations in air pollution epidemiology studies.

Figure 1. Relations between air pollution and health effects. Examples for potential points of influence of socioeconomic factors in italics.

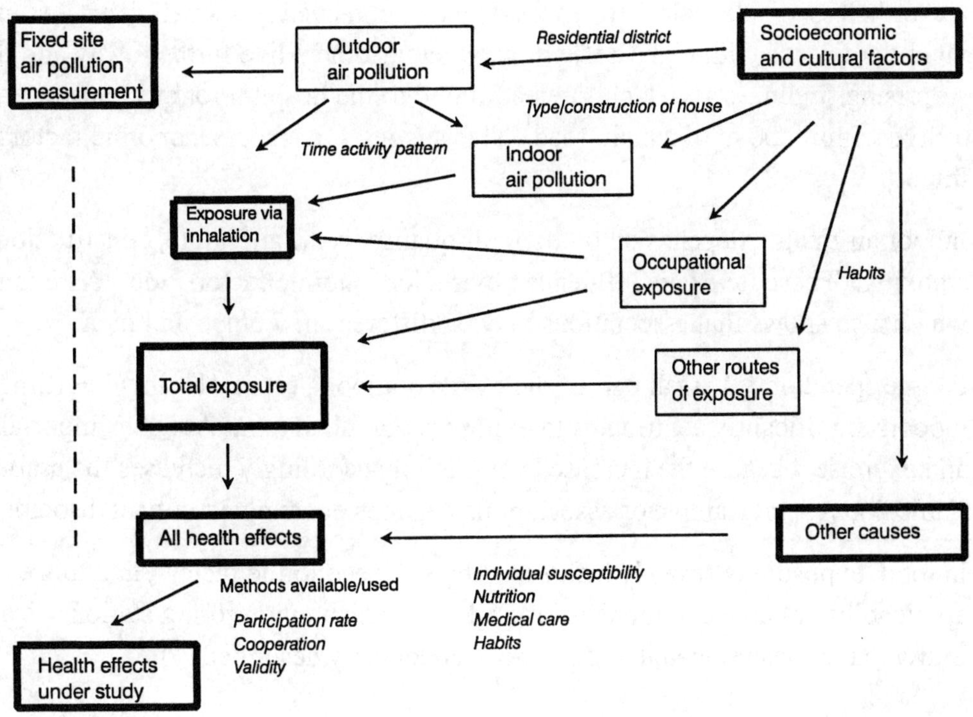

21

In general, we want to establish relations between exposure via inhalation on the one hand and health effects on the other hand. In practice, the health effects under study are only part of the existing health effects, and results of fixed site air pollution monitoring stations are far from being able to reflect the inhaled exposures of even those individuals living in the vicinity of the respective monitoring station. Thus, neither the estimates of exposure nor those of effects are generally able to reflect reality adequately and completely, and socioeconomic factors are an important reason for this fact.

INFLUENCE OF SOCIOECONOMIC FACTORS

Exposure

If a relation does exist between exposure and health effects, then exposure has to be understood as the total exposure of an individual, which consequently comprises not only exposure via inhalation, but also oral or dermal exposure. Occupational exposure often contributes to a significant amount to the total exposure. Exposure via inhalation is determined by outdoor and indoor air pollution and by the time spent in the respective micro-environments, and by ventilation rate depending on physical activity.

Monitoring stations can give a realistic picture of air pollution in their direct vicinity, but the concentrations vary with the distance from the station, with the height above ground, with the structure of the surroundings (houses, streets, trees, ...).

People live in certain districts of a town, and everybody knows that there are "better" and "worse" districts, not only with respect to the reputation, but also with respect to the costs of housing and largely with respect to air pollution. Thus, socioeconomic factors are directly linked with outdoor air pollution exposure ("... in this sample, the industrial core has the highest prevalence of gas stove use, smoking in the home, parental cough, chest illness in siblings, hospitalization for respiratory disease in infancy, crowding, low income, and low occupational status, as well as the highest air pollution levels." (1)).

Ambient air quality in a certain district may be sufficiently described by a local monitoring station. Nevertheless, small scale differences do exist, e.g. even in a small district some people live in the vicinity of roads with high traffic flow, whereas others live further away and thus inhale better air ("A surprising finding was that children admitted to the hospital for any cause were significantly more likely to live within 200 m of a main road. This suggests that socioeconomic factors might indeed be important, ..." (2)).

Indoor air quality depends on outdoor air quality, ventilation rate, construction of the houses, habits, and smoking. These items are influenced by socioeconomic factors, too. An example is given in table 1, which also shows that associations may be different in women and men.

People spend only a small part of their time outdoors, especially in wintertime, and the time spent indoors significantly contributes to exposure via inhalation. Another important factor is physical activity and exercise, because the increased ventilation accordingly increases the amounts of pollutants inhaled. Table 2 gives an example of associations between sporting activity and socioeconomic status.

In total, exposure is strongly influenced by socioeconomic factors, and this especially affects the applicability of concentrations measured by fixed site monitoring stations as a proxy of "real" exposure. Individual exposure via inhalation is not adequately described using fixed site air pollution measurement results, and socioeconomic factors considerably determine the degree of exposure misclassification.

Table 1:   School education and smoking (%) in the German population (3)

Sample size	school education		
	primary	secondary	higher
2265 men	43.1	42.6	34.9
2453 women	25.6	30.0	29.6

Table 2:   School education and regular sporting activity (%) in the German population (3)

Sample size	school education		
	primary	secondary	higher
2155 men	54.6	75.4	84.9
2297 women	44.3	74.1	79.3

Exposure and health outcome

If relations between total exposure and health effects really exist in the situation studied, they may be influenced by individual susceptibility, medical care, nutrition, and other habits with effects on general health. Socioeconomic factors can modify these conditions. It is likely that a small amount of additional stress is better tolerated by somebody who is healthy than by somebody being in a bad physical and/or mental condition. On the other hand, hay fever (as described, e.g. for Switzerland (4)) or perhaps asthma (e.g. for a British national sample (5)) are examples showing that associations between socioeconomic factors and individual susceptibility may also occur in an "unexpected" way, i.e. higher socioeconomic status may be linked with a higher prevalence of these diseases.

Health effects under study

The methods used to record health outcome depend on the availability and on the acceptance of the methods. Participation rate is influenced not only by the methods used, but also by socioeconomic factors, which may result in a selection bias. Participation rates are often higher in districts with higher socioeconomic status. Table 3 gives an example from Berlin.

In studies, which need intense cooperation by the participants, e.g. keeping a diary during a long period of time, accuracy of recording and thus the validity of records depends on socioeconomic factors, too. Even the classification of an effect, e.g. with respect to the severity of symptoms, is not independent from socioeconomic influences. Thus, socio-economic factors may lead to effect misclassification.

APPLICATION

As described above, socioeconomic factors may lead to exposure misclassification, biased dose-response relationship, and effects misclassification. Therefore, socioeconomic factors have to be adequately included in air pollution epidemiology studies.

Table 3: School education and participation rate (%) in different districts of Berlin (West) in a study of croup syndrome (6)

	Participation rate	School education of mother	
	(questionnaire)	lower	higher
Zone I	26	85	14
Zone II	32	77	23
Zone III	38	72	28

Temporal studies using aggregated data (Time-series studies)

Studies on mortality: Regarding the effects side, mortality studies have no problems with participation rate, cooperation and validity, because these data are generally available and not subject to voluntary decisions of the participants (this refers to the fact of death, i.e. total mortality; the reliability of causal diagnoses given in death certificates is substantially lower and at least partly associated with socioeconomic factors). Exposure assessment, however, is influenced by socioeconomic factors, because the information necessary to model exposure cannot be collected on an individual basis. Thus, exposure-effect relationships based on temporal studies using aggregated data necessarily suffer from a certain degree of exposure misclassification.

For administrative purposes, it sounds reasonable to establish relations between outdoor concentrations and mortality. A review and meta analysis of air pollution and daily mortality describes a relative risk of 1.06 for a 100 $\mu g/m^3$ increase in TSP concentration (7). Socioeconomic factors are not directly included in this analysis, but there seem to be no differences between studies in different regions with presumably different socioeconomic conditions. Neither seem there to be any differences between summer and winter exposures, in spite of the expected different percentages of time spent outdoors and different indoor/outdoor relations of pollutants concentrations.

Hospital admissions: The same aspects concerning exposure as mentioned above for mortality studies are to be mentioned with respect to studies on hospital admissions. In addition, there is a certain margin on the effects side, for the individual decision to accept hospital admission or not, which might be influenced by socioeconomic factors and thus might change the slope of the dose-response relationship found in a study. Therefore, socioeconomic status as a confounding factor is of greater importance than in mortality studies, but in practice consideration of socioeconomic factors is usually restricted to caveats in the discussions of results (2,8).

Cross-sectional studies using aggregated data

"Concentrations of air pollutants are usually higher in urban than in rural areas, and many authors have noted that smoking patterns, family size, age distribution, occupation, domestic crowding, nutrition, physical activity and other characteristics of the population can differ between rural and urban areas." (9). Authors try to adjust data, but "nevertheless, it is likely that the effects of variables such as personal habits, occupational exposure, and medical care cannot be fully quantified and eliminated in this way" (9).

Studies using individual data

Panel studies: Panel studies have the advantage that information on socioeconomic factors is usually available. This provides an opportunity to better model personal exposure. In addition, cooperation and validity of records can be judged. So problems with exposure and effects misclassification can be minimized (but not totally eliminated). Early studies using simple but effective methods, e.g. diary techniques, have been done in the UK (10).

The available range of exposure can be extended in coordinated studies in several countries with different patterns and concentrations of air pollutants. On the other hand, comparability of socioeconomic factors is more difficult in this case, as can be seen in current European studies such as the PEACE study. To generalize results to the general population, however, is difficult for several reasons, not only because panels usually consist of susceptible individuals.

Case-control studies: Case-control studies generally run the risk of exposure misclassification and selection bias. For both difficulties, socioeconomic factors are important and have to be considered carefully.

CONCLUSIONS

One way to improve air pollution epidemiology studies is to better include socioeconomic factors for reducing exposure and effect misclassification and confounding. Growing experience and improved statistical methods open possibilities to do so in all stages of studies from study design to analysis and understanding of results.

REFERENCES

1. Pengelly LD, Kerigan AT, Goldsmith CH, and Inman EM. The Hamilton Study: Distribution of Factors Confounding the Relationship between Air Quality and Respiratory Health. *JAPCA* 1984; **34**: 1039-1043.
2. Edwards J, Walters S, Griffiths RK. Hospital Admissions for Asthma in Preschool Children: Relationship to Major Roads in Birmingham, United Kingdom. *Archives of Environmental Health* 1994; **49**: 223-227.
3. Hoffmeister H, Hüttner H, Stolzenberg H, Lopez H, Winkler J. Sozialer Status und Gesundheit. bga-Schriften 2/92. MMV Verlag, München, 1992.
4. Wüthrich B, Schneyder UW, Henauer SA, Heller A. Häufigkeit der Pollinosis in der Schweiz. *Schweiz Med Wochenschr* 1986; **116**: 909-917.
5. Kaplan BA and Mascie-Taylor CGN. Asthma and Wheezy Bronchitis in a British National Sample. *Journal of Asthma* 1987; **24**: 289-296.

6. Englert N, König R, Prescher KE, Rodriguez-Hauschild E, Saal A, Seifert B. Obstruktive Bronchitis und Luftqualität in Berlin (West). Institut für Wasser-, Boden- und Lufthygiene des Bundesgesundheitsamtes. WaBoLu-Hefte 4/1989. Berlin, 1989.

7 . Schwartz J. Air pollution and Daily Mortality: A Review and Meta Analysis. *Environmental Research* 1994; **64**: 36-52.

8. Delfino RJ, Becklake MR, and Hanley JA. The Relationship of Urgent Hospital Admissions for Respiratory Illnesses to Photochemical Air Pollution Levels in Montreal. *Environmental Research* 1994; **67**: 1-19.

9. Ware JH, Thibodeau LA, Speizer FE, Colome S, and Ferris BG Jr. Assessment of the Health Effects of Atmospheric Sulfur Oxides and Particulate Matter: Evidence from Observational Studies. *Environmental Health Perspectives* 1981; **41**: 255-276.

10. Lawther PJ, Waller RE, and Henderson M. Air pollution and exacerbations of bronchitis. *Thorax* 1970; **25**: 525-539.

EVALUATION OF SOCIOECONOMIC FACTORS IN RESPIRATORY EPIDEMIOLOGY.

Laura Carrozzi

University and Hospital of Pisa, 2nd Division of Internal Medicine, and
CNR Institute of Clinical Physiology Via Paolo Savi 8, I-56124 Pisa, Italy

SUMMARY

An association between socioeconomic status (SES) and respiratory symptoms has been established in the literature of the last 30 years. Several authors have found lower lung function and higher prevalence of COPD in low SES. Results about asthma have been more contradictory. We performed a prospective study on the natural history of COPD using a multistage, stratified by SES and age, family clusters design. SES was defined (in two different stages) by 'crowding' and by 'percentage of heads of households in higher job positions'. An agreement between sampling SES characterization and information derived from the individual questionnaires of participants was found. Prevalence of respiratory symptoms was in general higher in subjects with lower SES characteristics; however, some differences were present considering the different variables to define SES. In conclusion, SES remains an important factor in respiratory epidemiology: discussion is still open regard to the use and the meaning of the different indicators.

INTRODUCTION

Socioeconomic status (SES) is correlated with mortality and morbidity of chronic diseases (1- 3). The purpose of this paper is to show an overview of the literature concerning the association between SES and chronic respiratory disease, in particular Chronic Obstructive Pulmonary Disease (COPD) and asthma, pointing out some open problems about the meaning of this relationship and the methodology of SES evaluation on respiratory epidemiology. In addition will be described how SES has been considered in the epidemiological prospective study on the natural history of COPD, performed by our group in the Po River Delta area (North Italy) (4).

As summarized in Table 1, few epidemiological studies of the last 30 years have considered SES as risk factor for COPD (5, 6). An association between low SES and lower values of lung function has been confirmed by different authors (7, 8). In some surveys prevalence of respiratory symptoms (9) and COPD (10) have also been evaluated and SES has been considered as a risk factor, along with smoking (which remains of overwhelming importance).

In the same period, Lebowitz (11) suggested an inverse relationship between income and most respiratory symptoms and COPD, although he did not find a significant relationship with asthma or productive cough. A similar inverse relationship was also found between education and prevalence rates of both COPD and severe productive cough. On the other hand, the author found occupational status to be only weakly related to any of the respiratory symptoms and diseases. No significant correlation was found between prevalence rates of various symptoms and a dichotomous SES index developed using variables such as income, education, and occupation. The importance of this paper is also in the methodological consideration that in the analysis of COPD data each SES variable must be considered as an independent factor and one should not combine them into a single overall SES index.

Table 1.   Socioeconomic status and COPD and asthma: Literature review

---

Holland, W.W. *et al.*, BMJ, 1969	Negative association with low SES and lung function (PEF)
Stebbings, J.H. *et al.*, Envir Res, 1971	Negative association with low SES and lung function (FEV_1)
Hrubec, Z. *et al.*, Arch Envir Health, 1973	Positive association of low SES with respiratory symptoms prevalence
Higgins, M.W. *et al.*, Am Rev Respir Dis, 1977	Association with disease in lower SES (COPD prevalence and negative lung function)(FEV_1)
Lebowitz M.D., J Chron Dis, 1977	Association with symptoms/disease prevalence
Smith, G.D. *et al.*, J Epid Comm Health, 1990	Higher mortality in low SES, also after control for smoking
Kanner, R.E. *et al.*, Am J Med, 1983	Positive correlation with survival probability
Egbuonu L., *et al.*, Pediatrics, 1982	Review; contradictory results on Asthma incidence, prevalence and severity
Anderson, H.R. *et al.*, Lancet, 1981	Association with maternal status and asthma prevalence
Weitzman, M.D.*et al.*, Am J Dis Ch, 1990	Association with SES and asthma prevalence
Martinez, F.D. et al., Pediatrics, 1992	Association of asthma incidence with low SES in smoking mothers

---

Both mortality and survival analyses have shown the importance of SES in relation to chronic respiratory diseases: mortality data controlled for smoking habit has shown that, while the higher prevalence of smoking was found among subjects in low SES, it was not a sufficient explanation for their increased mortality (13). About survival, subjects in the lower classes (according to job position) had a lower 12-year survival regardless the level of the airflow limitation (14).

In more recent years, few papers have analysed, in particular, the association between asthma in children and social status. It is generally believed that there is a higher prevalence of asthma among children in families of high socio economic status (15). Analysing parents interviews, asthma was more frequently reported by the 'not manual labor' social classes (16) and by subjects in high SES (17). These studies rely heavily on parental reporting of the presence of asthma and may reflect no more than enhanced parental recognition of the condition. Families of the lower social class may have less access to medical care and less confidence to the diagnosis and therefore they may not report the condition.

On the other hand, some researchers have found no significant relationship between incidence of asthma and social class (18), while others, reported an excess of severe asthma among children in low SES (19 - 21). The latter results are in agreement with a review on health conditions of children in which higher prevalence, increased severity and impact of illness among poor children, as defined by family income, was pointed out (22). The possible explanations were different: Anderson, in a study on the use of drugs for the treatment of wheezing among children (20), concluded that the effect of social class seemed to be explained by its association with the mother's mental status. Weitzman (21), analysing data on 15 416 children with a specific question related to social or socio- economic differences in rates of childhood asthma, concluded that black or poor children in the USA do have higher rates of asthma, that social and environmental factors exert substantial influences on rates of asthma, and that much of the social and economic disparity in prevalence can be accounted for by a variety of social and environmental characteristics.

Martinez *et al..* (23) found that there was no association between maternal smoking and subsequent incidence of asthma or maximal mid expiratory flow values among children of mothers with more than 12 years of education. They concluded that children of lower socioeconomic status may be at considerable risk of developing asthma if their mothers smoke 10 or more cigarettes per day.

MATERIAL AND METHODS

We analyzed our method of considering SES in Po Delta study on the natural history for COPD. This is an epidemiological prospective study, conducted twice, in the 1980-82 and in 1988-91, on a general population sample (n=3,289) living in an unpolluted rural area in the Northern Italy. Sampling was a multistage, stratified, by SES and age, family clusters design (4, 24).

The stratification by SES and age was carried out according to the sampling protocol of the Special Project of Chronic Obstructive Lung Disease of the Italian Research Council (4). This protocol used two SES indices for stratification. 1) "Crowding": the number of subjects living in the house divided by the number of rooms, and 2) the percentage of heads of households in higher occupational positions based on the official classification of Italian National Statistics Institute (ISTAT), i.e., white-collar workers, self-employed, professionals and managers (25, 26). On the basis of the distribution of these indices we obtained three SES strata: 'high', 'medium' and 'low'. The age stratification was performed on the basis of the age of heads of households. In the first stage of the sampling, census sections in the villages were selected in each geographic area according to their stratification by the first SES index. In the second stage, blocks within census section (about 50 families in each) were characterized by the second SES index and the age index, and were matched by strata and geographic zones. Specific blocks were chosen to represent their strata. Then, families in the blocks were randomly selected.

In the first survey of the study (which these results refer to) subjects completed the standardized CNR questionnaire on respiratory symptoms and risk factors (27) and performed lung function tests. In the second survey, bronchial reactivity, atopy and some biological markers were also evaluated.

RESULTS

There were no differences between participants and non-participants for age and SES stratification index; instead, there were statistically significant differences for sex, because 48% of participants were males vs 58% of non-participants, and for job position, because a larger number of non-working population was included among the participants than among the non-participants (4).

In order to verify the efficiency of our sampling design, socioeconomic characteristics of participants collected by questionnaire were compared among the three SES strata defined according to the sampling design (Table 2). There was a substantial agreement between SES characterization from the sampling design and questionnaire information (27). In fact, for instance regarding job position, there were higher percentages of blue-collars and unemployed in low SES, higher percentage of people with no education in low SES, and, conversely, higher percentage of people with more than 13 years of education in high SES. Regarding housing conditions almost all houses of high SES had bathroom inside, whereas 6% of houses in low SES had bathroom outside. Again, 80% of houses in high SES had heating in all rooms; instead, 44% of houses in low SES did not have heating in all rooms. As regards crowding index, it was in agreement with anticipated SES characteristics: in fact, its mean value ranged from 1.13 persons per room in low SES to 0.93 in high SES.

Table 2.   **Socioeconomic characteristics of participants, from questionnaire information, in the three SES strata.**

	LOW (%)	MID (%)	HIGH (%)	p
JOB POSITION				
Blue-collars	29.2	27.4	25.2 (*	
Self-employed	14.9	11.7 (*	15.4	
White-collars	4.8 (*	9.4	11.6 (*	<.001($
Prof. & Mgr. (°	0.5 (*	1.2	2.9	
Unemployed	50.6	50.3	44.9 (*	
EDUCATION				
No educ.	23.5 (*	20.6	15.8 (*	
5 years	39.1	41.1	40.2	<.001 ($
8 years	27.1	25.7	25.9	
<13 years	10.2 (*	12.6 (*	18.1 (*	
HOUSE CONDITIONS				
No bathroom	6.4 (*	1.0	0.4 (*	<.01 ($
Bathroom (°°	93.6 (*	99.0	99.6 (*	
No heating	43.7 (*	21.8	19.5 (*	<.001 ($
Heating (°°°	56.3 (*	78.2	80.5 (*	

	m	SD	m	SD	m	SD	p
'Crowding'	1.13	.49	1.00	.85	.93	.54	<.01 ($$

°) Professionals and Managers; °°) presence of complete bathroom inside; °°°) presence of heating in all rooms; $) by chi-square test ; $$) by ANOVA; *) significant by adjusted residuals analysis.

On the basis of these results, we analyzed respiratory symptoms assessed in the first survey in relation to some SES characteristics derived from individual questionnaires (education, occupation) and in relation to the sampling SES index. Prevalence of symptoms were, in general, higher in those in lower socioeconomic level; the results were more evident in smokers and considering, separately, occupation (Fig. 1) or education, instead of the 'sampling' variable.

DISCUSSION

Looking at the literature review (Table 1) we can conclude that SES remains an important factor in respiratory diseases and must be considered in respiratory epidemiology. However a still open question is to clarify the mechanism underlying this association: in particular is the association present *per se* or as indicator of other factors?

In relation to COPD, according to the comments of some of these authors (10), possible explanations include differences between the groups in reporting symptoms, or in obtaining medical care, differences in understanding and responding to instructions for lung function tests, differences in exposure to acute respiratory infections or air pollution, and differences directly related to SES. These considerations are evident considering the different ways of classifying SES (income, education, occupation). These variables are correlated with a variety of experiences and behaviours that may be relevant to the occurrence of chronic respiratory diseases.

Smoking habits are very important in this connection (10, 23): when smoking was taken into account, the effect of poor socioeconomic circumstances tended to be more pronounced among smokers than among nonsmokers. It is possible that this greater apparent association reflects a greater susceptibility of the lung to damage when exposed to smoking and other harmful conditions related to SES.

Another important consideration regards the different results of the different SES variables in relation to the evidence of diseases. Occupational status was related less closely to prevalence rates of symptoms or disease than income or education; in addition, income can differ from education (11).

Our results on the comparison between sampling SES classification and information collected by questionnaire showed a sufficient efficiency of our SES index. However, as also shown in the paper of Viegi (28), the association between our respiratory outcomes and SES was less strong considering the single SES index than the separate variables (particularly education and occupation). As described by Viegi, SES indicators in our sample were correlated with other risk factors: occupational exposure, housing conditions, and environmental tobacco smoke. These findings confirmed the hypothesis of the different effect of income and education on health, on perception of health and on medical care sought and received.

About asthma, results were contradictory. Although it is generally believed that there was a higher prevalence of asthma among children in families of higher socio economic status (15), low level of mother's education is associated with higher prevalence or severity of the disease (20, 21). Also in this case the effect could be related to parental behaviour (for example, smoking at home) or to 'cultural' approach to the disease prevention and therapy.

The considerations about the relationship between SES and COPD or Asthma, confirm that the effect of social factors on respiratory disease prevalence and severity is strongly related to environmental characteristics. Thus it must be taken into account as an important confounder in the research on the effect of the environmental and respiratory health.

ACKNOWLEDGEMENT

This work was supported in part by the National Research Council, Targeted Project "Prevention and Control of Disease Factors - SP2 - Contract N° 91.00171.PF41"; the CNR-ENEL Project "Interactions of the Energy System with Human Health and Environment", Rome, Italy; the Contract No. BMH1-CT92-0849 (BIOMED1) between the European Economic Community and the University of Pisa, Italy; Boehringer Ingelheim Italia.

REFERENCES

1. Marmot MG, Kogevinas M, Elston MA. Socioeconomic Status and Disease. *WHO Reg Publ Eur Ser* 1991; **37**: 113-146.
2. Kogevinas M, Marmot MG, Fox AJ, Goldblatt PO. Socioeconomic Differences in Cancer Survival. *J Epidemiol Community Health*, 1991; **45**: 216-219.
3. Graham S, Reeder LG. Social Epidemiology of Chronic Disease. In Freeman H., Levine S., Reeder L.G., eds Handbook of medical sociology. Englewood Cliffa, N.J.: Prentice-Hall, 1979.
4. Carrozzi L, Giuliano G, Viegi G, Paoletti P, Di Pede F, Mammini U, Saracci R, Giuntini C, Lebowitz MD. The Po river delta epidemiological study of obstructive lung disease: sampling methods, environmental and population characteristics. *European Journal of Epidemiology* 1990; **6**: 191-200.
5. Krzyzanowski M, Jedrychowski W, Wysocki M. Factors Associated with the Change in Ventilatory Function and the Development of Chronic Obstructive Pulmonary Disease in a 13-years Follow-up of the Cracow Study. Risk of Chronic Obstructive Pulmonary Disease. *Am Rev Respir Dis* 1986; **134**: 1011-1010.
6. Sherrill D.L., Lebowitz M.D., Burrows B.. Epidemiology of Chronic Obstructive Pulmonary Disease. *Clinics in Chest Medicine*, 1990; **11**: 375-387.
7. Holland WW, Halil T, Bennet RE, Elliot A. Factors influencing the onset of chronic respiratory disease. *BMJ* 1969; **2**: 205-208.
8. Stebbings JH. Chronic Respiratory Disease among nonsmokers in Hagerstown, Maryland.III. Social class and Chronic Respiratory Disease. *Envir Res* 1971; **4**: 213-232.
9. Hrubec Z, Cederlof R, Friberg L. Respiratory Symptoms in Twins. Effect of Residence-associated Air Pollution, Tobacco and Alcohol use, and other factors. *Arch Environ Health* 1973, **277**: 189-195.
10. Higgins MW, Keller JB, Metzrener HL . Smoking, Socioeconomic Status and Chronic Respiratory Disease. *Am Rev Respir Dis* 1977; **116**: 403-410.
11. Lebowitz MD. The Relationship of Socio-Environmental Factors to the Prevalence of Obstructive Lung Diseases and Other Chronic Conditions. *J Chron Dis* 1977; **30**: 599-611.
12. Antonovsky A. Social class and cardiovascolar diseases. *J Chron Dis* 1968; **21**: 65-106.
13. Smith GD, Shipley MJ, Rose G. Magnitude and Causes of Socioeconomic differentials in mortality: further evidence from the Whitehall Study. *J Epidemiol and Community Health* 1990; **44**: 265-270.
14. Kanner RE, Renzetti AD, Stanish W, Barkman HW, Klauber MR. Predictors of Survival in Subjects with Chronic Airflow Limitation. *Am J Med*, 1983; **74**: 249-255.
15. Mitchell EA, Stewart AW, Pattermore PK, Asher MI, Harrison AC, Rea HH. Socioeconomic status in childhood asthma. *Int J Epidemiol* 1989; **18**: 888-890.
16. Peckham C, Butler N. A National Study of Asthma in Childhood. *J Epidemiol Community Health* 1978; **32**: 79-85.
17. Graham PJ, Rutter ML, Yule M, Pless IB. Childhood Asthma: A Psychosomatic Disorder? *Br J Prev Soc Med* 1967: **21**:78-85.
18. McNichol KN, Williams HE, Allan J, McAndrew I. Spectrum of Asthma in Children.III. Psychological and social components. *BMJ* 1973; **4**: 16-20.
19. Mitchell RG, Dawson B. Educational and Social Characteristics of Children with Asthma. *Arch Dis Child*, 1973; **48**: 467-471.
20. Anderson HR, Bailey PA, Cooper JS, Palmer JC. Influence of Morbidity, Illness Label, and Social, Family, and Health Service Factors on Drug Treatment of Childhood Asthma. *Lancet*, 1981; **7**: 1030-1032.
21. Weitzman MD, Gortmaker S, Sobol A. Racial, Social, and Environmental Risks for Childhood Asthma. *AJCD*, 1990; **144**: 1189-1194.
22. Egbuonu L, Starfield. Child Health and Social Status. *Pediatrics*, 1982; 69: 550-557.

23. Martinez F, Cline M, Burrows B. Increased Incidence of Asthma in Children of Smoking Mothers . *Pediatrics*, 1992; **89**: 21-26.

24. Cochran WG. Sampling Techniques. New York, Wiley and Sons, 3rd ed. 1973

25. Istituto Centrale di Statistica (1977). XI Censimento Generale della Popolazione, Vol. XI, Atti del Censimento, Roma.24 Ottobre 1971.

26. Istituto Centrale di Statistica. Classificazione delle Attivita' Economiche. Metodi e norme: serie C, n. 5. Roma. 1971

27. Fazzi P, Viegi G, Paoletti P, Giuliano G, Begliomini E, Fornai E, Giuntini C. Comparison between Two Standardized Questionnaires and Pulmonary Function Tests in a Group of Workers. *Eur J Respir Dis* 1982; **63**: 168-169.

28. Viegi G. Effect of socioeconomic conditions on respiratory symptoms and lung function tests in two Italian community studies. In Jantunen MJ, Viegi G, Nolan C (Eds) *Socioeconomic and Cultural Factors in Air Pollution Epidemiology*. **EC Air Pollution Epidemiology Report Series No: 8,** 1997, 77-86.

INCORPORATION OF SOCIOECONOMIC AND CULTURAL FACTORS IN STUDY DESIGN AND DATA ANALYSIS

Ulrich Ranft

Medical Institute of Environmental Hygiene, Heinrich-Heine-University Düsseldorf,
Auf'm Hennekamp 50, D-40225 Düsseldorf, Germany

SUMMARY

Socioeconomic and cultural (SEC) factors are significant in air pollution epidemiology either as confounders or as modifiers. This paper presents a short overview of the main principles for dealing with confounding and interaction in study design and data analysis. Whereas interaction is model dependent and therefore not a bias, confounding needs special attention to avoid bias in estimating health effects of air pollution exposure. For various study types, such as the ecologic study, the cohort study or the case-control study, the confounder problem presents different aspects. Confounding must be considered already in the study design. Stratified analysis and mathematical modelling are used to control for confounders in data analysis. SEC factors are potential candidates for misclassification. Despite controlling for confounders with substantial misclassification in the data analysis, a bias, called residual confounding, will occur which is difficult to evaluate. New techniques helping in the case of nondifferential misclassification are mentioned.

CONFOUNDING

Air pollution epidemiology consists almost exclusively of nonexperimental epidemiology, i.e. nonrandomized assignment of study subjects to intervention or exposure groups. In nonexperimental epidemiologic research confounding is a central issue and terms an epidemiologic bias. An observable variable is a confounder if it fulfils the following requirements (1):

1. A confounder must be a risk factor for the disease (or health outcome), either causally related to or an indicator of increased risk of the disease, apart of its association with the exposure under study.
2. A confounder must be associated (correlated) with the exposure under study.
3. A confounder must not be an intermediate step in the causal pathway between the exposure and the disease.

A "working definition" calls a factor a confounder if its "control", often jointly with other variables, reduces or avoids a bias when estimating the health effect of the exposure under study. Typical potential confounders in environmental epidemiology are age, sex and smoking. Socioeconomic and cultural (SEC) factors are strong determinants of health in many epidemiologic studies, hence they should always be considered candidates for confounding in air pollution epidemiology.

INTERACTION

It is important to distinguish effect modification and interaction from confounding. When the observed effect of the exposure is different at different levels of another factor, this factor is an effect modifier. Effect modification is not a bias to be avoided, rather it is part of the relation between exposure and health outcome and can be an aspect of the study object itself. The analysis of modification depends on the way the relation between health outcome and its determinant is modelled. For example, by fitting a linear regression model to a data set, a factor may turn out to be an effect modifier, but in corresponding multiplicative (exponential) model this factor can simply be treated as a confounder.

In study design, to provide an assessment of interaction between the exposure under study and one or more other variables, one needs in general larger sample size and higher resolution of both the exposure variable and the potential modifiers. In data analysis the identification of specific effect modifying factors is recommended as one of the first steps before any consideration should be given to issues of confounding (2).

Interactions of air pollution with other factors in causing health effects are difficult to study, especially when SEC factors are considered. SEC factors are not causes of health effects, rather they are indicators of not directly observed risk factors or causal relations between the exposure and health outcome. Therefore, if in data analysis an SEC variable turns out to be an effect modifier, every effort should be made to reveal the underlying causal factor.

CONTROLLING FOR CONFOUNDERS

The primary task connected with the incorporation of SEC factors in study design and data analysis is to control for their potential confounding, i.e. to reduce or, preferably, avoid bias in estimating the effect of the exposure on the health outcome. The quantitative methods in epidemiologic research provide a large collection of effective instruments for dealing with confounding in study design and in data analysis (e.g. 2,3,4,5). Only crude overview of the main concepts in study design and data analysis can be given in the following. An important distinction of study types concerning confounding exists between "ecological design" and "basic observational design". In data analysis, for attacking the confounding problem, the application of both commonly used general approaches, stratified analysis as well as mathematical modelling, is recommended.

Ecologic Design

In ecologic or aggregate studies exposure levels and health data of groups instead of individuals are the units of observation and analysis. Although the ecologic design is widely used in environmental epidemiology because of its comparatively low cost, the interpretation of associations between aggregated exposure indicators and aggregated health data is difficult with respect to etiologic processes at the level of individuals. The methodological limitations in the use of ecologic data to estimate causal parameters are founded in the ecologic fallacy or ecologic bias. The ecologic bias should not be confused with confounding, although confounding can be the source of ecological bias (6). Even if a risk factor is unrelated to exposure status at individual level, i.e. it is not a confounder at individual level, differential distribution of the factor across groups may induce ecological bias. Somewhat misleading terms "confounding by group" or "effect modification by group" are used for this situation.

One method to control for extraneous risk factors in ecologic studies is to include distribution measures of these factors as terms in the model, e.g. proportion of an ethnic group or mean income in each ecologic unit. Nevertheless, sufficient removal of ecologic bias is often doubtful. In fact, bias may be increased after such adjustment. Rate standardization, often employed to adjust for age, is rarely applicable in case of SEC factors since it requires mutual standardization of all variables in the model for those confounding factors not included. For this the necessary information is usually not available.

Basic Observational Design

For three study types of the basic observational design, i.e. cross-sectional study, cohort study and case-control study, confounding is treated identically in many respects. In panel studies the confounding bias, from variables that represent individual risk factors without temporal variation, is usually insignificant or nonexisting because the individual is used as its own control.

For designing a study it is important to distinguish between conceptual entities of the phenomena to be observed and their empirical or operational counterparts. Accordingly, the socioeconomic status or the cultural background of a study subject are only concepts. Out of a set of empirical items one or several indices must be formed to measure the conceptual entity. This process of operationalization must take place in the design phase of the study, and not simply in the analysis, which means in the light of the data. The operationalization of SEC factors is often a difficult task when the concept itself is not well defined and SEC factors are used as surrogates for not directly observable risk factors. Misclassification occurs as a consequence of insufficient operational measures of SEC factors.

At the design stage the control of extraneous variables may be employed by some type of subject selection procedure. This selection could be either restriction or matching. Restriction provides an efficient control for confounding, if the range of admissibility is sufficiently narrow. But on the other hand, restriction makes statistical inference outside of the range of admissibility impossible and limits the external validity of the study. In air pollution epidemiology, for example, restriction of nationality, race, sex or age is often applied. The aim of matching is to make the reference group as similar as possible to the index group with respect to the distributions of the potential confounders. In case-control studies, matching does not exempt from controlling for confounders in the data analysis, but it improves precision of effect estimation. The use of frequency matching is good scientific standard for case-control studies. Pair matching is a special matching technique where each stratum of the potential confounders contains one index subject and one reference subject. This requires specific methods in data analysis.

Stratified Analysis

Preferably at the beginning of the analysis the relationship of health outcome and exposure should be studied in strata defined by one or several potential confounders. The appeal of stratification is the straightforward manner in which confounding or, if present, modifying effects of extraneous variables can be assessed. But stratification is severely restricted by the fast decreasing group size in each of the strata with increasing number of strata. In air pollution epidemiology usually a larger set of potential confounders has to be considered. Therefore, stratification analysis is helpful for obtaining a general impression of the confounding situation and, especially important, for detecting interaction in the data, but it is only a first step in data analysis.

Mathematical Modelling

The simultaneous control for a larger set of confounders in data analysis is only possible by mathematical modelling. Generalized linear models are the most commonly used approaches and their application is well supported by modern statistical program packages. In general, the mathematical model is the linear regression of the response variable y, or a function (link function) of y, on the exposure and confounder variables, z and x_i, respectively. The incorporation of effect modification, if necessary, is usually accomplished by addition of multiplicative terms:

$$f(y) = a + b z + \sum_i c_i x_i + [\_\sum_j d_j \, x_j z_j \,]$$

The independent variables of the model must be either continuous or dichotomous. SEC factors are usually measured in a categorical or ordinal scale. Therefore, a common practice is to introduce "dummy" variables, e.g. the n categories of a SEC factor are represented by n-1 dichotomous dummy variables (0/1-variables).

If the model is correct and no interaction must be included, the estimated regression coefficient b represents an unbiased estimation of the effect of the exposure variable z on the response variable y adjusted for the confounder variables x_i. The inclusion of confounders in the model is crucial for the unbiasedness of the estimations. However, unnecessary inclusion of regression variables, i.e. variables which are no confounders and no strong risk factors for the health outcome, reduces the statistical efficiency of the model, i.e. the precision in estimation.

The presence of confounding of an extraneous variable should never be assessed by a statistical test of its significance as a predictor in the model, but by the change in the effect measure due to adjusting for it in the model. In the literature many procedures are proposed to check for correctness of the model. Two important assumptions of the linear regression model should be examined in any case: the linearity of the relations and the independence of the residual error from the model variables. This can simply, but also effectively be done by evaluation of the residuals of the model, usually by graphical methods.

MISCLASSIFICATION

As mentioned above SEC factors used in epidemiological studies are only indicators or even 'proxies' for not directly observable conceptual phenomena. Therefore, even if SEC factors are measured correctly, the underlying conceptual phenomenon may be represented only with large measurement errors of systematic or random nature. Those measurement errors can imply a bias termed information bias. For categorical variables, such as SEC factors, a measurement error means misclassification. If the misclassification is related with the health outcome, then this is called differential misclassification, otherwise nondifferential.

Misclassification of confounders may produce serious problems in studying weak exposure-response relationships like in air pollution epidemiology. If we can assume a substantial nondifferential misclassification for a strong confounder, despite controlling for confounding in the data analysis, a bias will occur. That means, adjustment will not completely eliminate the bias due to the confounder. This bias is then called residual confounding and can be either towards or away from the null value. That is in contrast with nondifferential misclassification of the exposure which will only reduce the power of the study, i.e. the bias is towards the null value. Usually, more than one confounder with misclassification have to be considered simultaniously in a regression model. Consequently, the effect of residual confounding will be even more complex.

If an accurate method for measuring the confounder exists, but its application to a larger sample of subjects is prohibitively expensive or infeasible, a two-stage sampling design has been proposed (7). The less accurate measuring method is applied to the total study sample, whereas the more accurate one is used only for a subsample. If the misclassification of the less accurate method is nondifferential, estimation procedures for logistic regression models are available which combine the information from both samples. On one hand, the success of the two-stage sampling approach depends strongly on the fulfilment of its main prerequisites, i.e. nondifferential misclassification and representativity of the subsample. On the other hand, the potential residual confounding should be of sufficient magnitude to justify the expenditure of a two-stage sampling.

DISCUSSION

SEC factors have to be considered in air pollution epidemiology as risk factors on the health outcome, usually as indicators for causal factors not directly observable. Therefore, SEC factors are treated as either potential confounders or potential modifiers in the conventional manner that is well covered in many textbooks (e.g. 2,3,4,5). Two aspects of SEC factors are of special concern; the possibility of a nonstatistical relation between the exposure variable and the SEC factor, and possible misclassification. A causal relation between the exposure measure and the SEC factor may result in overcontrolling in the mathematical modelling and, therefore, in an underestimation of the health effects. The combination of 'residential area' as an exposure measure and 'income' as an indicator of the social status, for instance, can produce overcontrolling. As mentioned above, the effects of misclassification, even if nondifferential, on the risk estimates are difficult to assess because both overestimation and underestimation are possible.

Much experience is needed to appropriately incorporate SEC factors in air pollution epidemilology studies. Good experience in the mathematical-statistical methodology is mandatory, but close acquaintance with the practice and the results of air pollution epidemiology studies is also needed. The collection of examples given in this Report will provide a good basis, but further research is still strongly desirable.

REFERENCES

1. Katsouyanni K (ed.) Study Designs. Air Pollution Epidemiology Reports Series, Report Number 4. Commission of the European Communities. EUR 15095 EN, 1993
2. Kleinbaum DG, Kupper LL, Morgenstern H. Epidemiologic Research. Principles and Quantitative Methods. Wadsworth Inc., Belmont, California, 1982
3. Rothman KJ. Modern Epidemiology. Little and Brown, Boston, 1986
4. Miettinen OS. Theoretical Epidemiology. Principles of Occurrence Research in Medicine. Delmar Publishers Inc., New York, 1985
5. Breslow NE, Day NE. Statistical Methods in Cancer Research. Vol. I and II. International Agency for Research on Cancer, Lyon, 1980 and 1987
6. Morgenstern H, Thomas D. Principles of Study Design in Environmental Epidemiology. *Environmental Health Perspectives Supplements*, 1993; **101**, Suppl. 4, 23-38.
7. Schill W et al. Logistic analysis in case-control studies under validation sampling. *Biometrika*, 1993;**80**, 339-352.

COMPARISON OF THE INFLUENCE OF SOCIOECONOMIC FACTORS ON AIR POLLUTION HEALTH EFFECTS IN WEST AND EAST GERMANY

Ursula Krämer[1], L. Altmann[1], H. Behrendt[2], R. Dolgner[1], M.S. Islam[1], H.G. Kaysers[1], J. Ring[2], R. Stiller-Winkler[3], M. Turfeld[1], M. Weishoff-Houben[4], H. Willer[5], G. Winneke[1]

[1] Medical Institute of Environmental Hygiene, Auf'm Hennekamp 50, D-40225 Düsseldorf
[2] Department of Dermatology, University Hamburg, Martinistr. 52, D-20246 Hamburg
[3] Institute of Hygiene, Heinrich-Heine University, Universitätsstr. 1, D-40225 Düsseldorf
[4] Institute of Hygiene and Environmental Medicine, University Aachen, Pauwelsstr. 30, D-52074 Aachen
[5] State Institute of Hygiene, Wallonerberg 2/4, D-39104 Magdeburg

INTRODUCTION

Since the nineteenth century is has been known that there is a relation between social class and health status [1]. In our study on school beginners on air pollution health effects in West and East Germany 1991 [2] a lot of health endpoints ranging from internal body load over functional impairments to airway diseases and allergies had been investigated. It seemed worthwhile to look whether the well known fact that the higher classes generally are healthier [1] could be reproduced with our data, too. The first aim of this presentation therefore is to examine the association between health effects measures and social class in a systematic way.

Most often social class is considered as a potential confounder [1], because of its strong association to exposure as well as to health effects. The amount of such a potential confounding is demonstrated with the data on school beginners, too.

Since parental education is never a direct cause of a functional change or a change in disease status residual confounding may always be present. Primary risk factors should be looked for. Examples of this will be given, too.

In the western industrialized cities income, occupation and education which constitute "social class" are usually highly correlated. When determining the effects of education you can-not be sure whether the seen effects have to be ascribed to income difference, too. As the relation between income, occupation and education was much less pronounced in the GDR than in the BRD, a comparison of the influence of education on health effects should allow to disentangle life style effects (connected with education) from merely economic effects. Our study gives the unique opportunity to make such a comparison since it took place 3 months after the German unification, when the economic changes in East Germany just began. We therefore assume that differences between groups characterized by parental education, reflect differences that have been built up during the former GDR and FRG periods.

METHODS

Study Areas

The areas in East Germany were chosen to represent a range of different air-pollution levels. Halle and Leipzig are industrialized cities in Saxony and Saxony-Anhalt, Magde-burg is the capital of Saxony-

Anhalt with comparatively moderate pollution, and in the Altmark three small district capitals Salzwedel, Gardelegen and Osterburg were included.

The areas in Nordrein-Westfalen were suggested by the clean-air plans (Luftreinhaltepläne) of that state. They are parts of Duisburg, Essen, Gelsenkirchen, Dortmund which are industrialized towns in the Ruhr area and Borken which is a small district capital north of the Ruhr area.

Study Design, subjects and response

Cross-sectional studies have been repeated every year since 1991 in East Germany and every third year in West Germany. Here, only the design of the 1991 study is given. All boys and girls entering the elementary school in 1991 and living in the geographically defined areas were chosen. A letter was mailed to the parents asking for participation of the child and for completion of a questionnaire at home, to be checked by a physician on the day of the medical examination immediately following the health check-up compulsory for all first graders. The staff of the local health departments collected blood and urine specimen from all children in predefined subareas of the cities. Blood and serum were deep-frozen and analyzed in one laboratory. All studies took place in the spring of 1991. 4074 children in East Germany participated in the questionnaire study (response rate 93%) and 4865 in West Germany (response rate 78%).

Neuropsychological tests were done with a computer-administered test battery by one team in Leipzig, Gardelegen and Duisburg. Additionally visual evoked potentials were measured under three stimulus conditions. 361 children (about every third in the predefined areas) participated. This part of the study is named the "neuro-study". A detailed description of the used methods can be found in [3].

One team in a mobile lung-function laboratory did body plethysmographic measurements. Due to time constraints children from Gardelegen, Gelsenkirchen and Dortmund were not included. 1323 children out of the predefined subareas participated, these were 93% of those who completed a questionnaire and were chosen to participate. This part of the study is referred to as the "lung-study". Detailed information about the methods are in [4].

Dermatological tests were done by physicians of one clinic in Halle, Duisburg, Essen and Borken. 1273 (= 87% of those who completed a questionnaire) participated. In the just mentioned areas, as well as in all East German areas, blood samples for the analysis of specific IgE were gathered. The subgroup of 2323 German children who underwent dermatological tests or gave blood for the analysis of specific IgE makes up the so-called "allergy-study". More methodological details of this study are given in [5].

Assessment of education

The school-systems in the GDR and in the FRG were fairly different. Years of schooling seemed to be the most comparable indicator. The school years of the better educated parent were taken to characterize the family. Four groups were built
- 1: leaving school before the 10th grade
- 2: leaving school with the 10th grade
- 3: leaving school with the final exam (12 years in East Germany and 13 years in West Germany) without academic education
- 4: academic education

Especially the first level is not quite comparable. In the GDR it was quite unusual to leave school before the 10th grade.

Table 1.   **Health outcome variables and methods of their assessment**

Concentrations of harmful substances	**in blood:** **in teeth:** **in urine:**	lead, cadmium lead, cadmium arsenic, mercury, cadmium, *method: AAS*
Functional parameters	**immune reaction:** **allergological parameters:** **lung function:** **neurophysiology:** **neuropsychology:**	immunoglobulins (A, E, G, M), complement components (C3c, C4), *method: nephelometry* IgE-antibodies (birch/ mugwort/ grass pollen, house dust mite, food) *method: CAP RAST* skin prick test, atopic eczema *method: examination by dermatologists* airway resistance (R_{AW}) intrathoracic gas volume (ITGV) *method: bodyplethysmography* latency of visual evoked potentials test of tapping speed, visual retention, pattern comparison, and reaction time *method: NES1 test batterie*
Symptoms and diagnoses of airway diseases and allergic manifestations	**in the last 12 months:** **ever diagnosed**	number of colds, tonsillitis, dry cough, frequently running nose, reddened eyes, attacks of sneezing, swellings pseudocroup, pneumonia, bronchitis, asthma, hay-fever, eczema *method: questionnaire*

Statistical evaluation

For all health effects the raw associations to education were determined for the data from East and West German separately. Education with the four levels described above was treated as quantitative and was introduced as dependent variable in a linear (quantitative effects) or logistic regression model (binary effects). Significance tests were used in a merely descriptive manner to decide what associations should be investigated in more detail. For this decision a p value of at least 0.1 has to be reached.

RESULTS

Harmful substances in blood, teeth or urine

Lead in blood and teeth showed a strong association with parental education, stronger in East than in West Germany. The geometric mean values were higher for children with lower educated parents. Mean values for blood lead are given in Table 2 for the neuro-study. No concentrations of any other measured substances in blood, teeth or urine were related to education.

43

Table 2. Mean values (percentage of positive values for allergy study) of exposure and health outcome variables in subgroups of children with differently educated parents.

Parents' years of schooling	West Germany				East Germany			
	<10	=10	=13	academic	<10	=10	=12	academic
Neuro-Study[1]: n	14	45	32	22	18	85	83	40
PB in blood x_g [µg/dl]	5.4	5.2	4.4	4.5	8.9	6.4	6.0	5.3
s_g	1.5	1.5	1.3	1.2	1.5	1.5	1.5	1.5
visual retention x_g [n correct]	4.8	4.9	5.5	5.2	4.4	4.5	4.8	5.5
s_g	1.5	1.6	1.4	1.5	1.3	1.6	1.5	1.6
Lung-Study[2]: n	74	102	54	51	56	426	315	186
ITGV[l] x_a	1.03	1.07	1.10	1.03	1.01	1.02	1.04	1.06
std	0.17	0.15	0.16	0.18	0.14	0.16	0.17	0.16
Allergy-Study[3]: ever diagnosed allergy	13.2	14.6	26.2	20.1	7.3	11.5	17.8	15.4
hay fever	1.7	1.2	4.7	1.6	0.0	1.2	1.5	3.0
bronch.asthma	0.9	0.9	2.6	1.1	2.1	1.2	0.9	1.5
eczema	6.1	9.7	15.8	19.1	9.4	13.0	17.7	19.5
n	116	340	190	183	96	593	454	272
Atop. eczema at the day of invest.	8.8	11.4	13.8	15.9	5.9	17.3	23.3	12.2
n	102	315	181	183	17	104	90	74
Ever wheezing	14.0	19.9	25.5	25.7	14.7	13.7	18.8	19.9
n	114	337	188	183	95	578	447	261
IgE antibodies against birch pollen	4.5	8.1	8.5	8.5	1.1	3.2	2.7	7.2
grass pollen	5.6	8.8	15.5	8.5	7.7	9.2	12.3	17.4
house-dust mite	9.0	9.2	13.4	15.7	13.2	8.3	10.1	12.8
any positive	13.5	21.5	24.7	22.3	24.2	19.7	26.6	28.7
n	89	261	142	153	91	589	447	265

[1]) x_g = geometric mean; s_g = geometric dispersion factor
[2]) x_a = arithmetic mean; **std** = standard deviation
[3]) **percentages**

Neurophysiological and neuropsychological functions

No association to education levels of parents could be seen for the measured latencies of visual evoked potentials, whereas the groups of children with higher educated parents exhibited better mean performance for the neuropsychological variables, with the exception of tapping. Table 2 gives the result of the visual retention test as an example. The geometric mean values of correctly identified patterns (maximum 12) differed by 1.1 point depending on the educational level of the parents. The association in East Germany was stronger than in West Germany.

The main goal of the neuro-study was to determine Pb-related functional impairments of the nervous system. The educational status of the parents is an important confounding variable in this context, because of its association both with neuropsychological outcome variables and with blood lead. The regression coefficient describing the relation between the number of correctly identified patterns and the concentration of lead in blood, measured in μg/dl, changed from -0.067 (s_b=0.043) to -0.035 (s_b=0.045), when education of parents was additionally included in the regression model.

Table 3. **Percentage of positive values (mean values) of possibly confounding factors (allergy study) with highest association to parental education.**

Parents' years of schooling	West Germany				East Germany			
	<10	=10	=13	academic	<10	=10	=12	academic
Perinatal health risks								
Smoking of mother in [%] pregnancy n	48.3 120	32.5 348	18.2 192	13.3 188	33.7 95	18.9 604	9.8 460	3.7 274
Birthweight[%] < 2500 g n	6.9 116	9.3 345	5.2 191	5.4 186	10.9 92	8.4 598	5.0 457	3.7 272
Breastfeed-[%] ing ≥ 2 month n	23.9 117	30.1 339	39.5 190	64.1 184	33.0 88	33.0 585	45.4 454	56.1 271
Characterisation of dwellings where children live								
Wall-to-wall carpet in sleeping [%] room of child n	86.4 118	88.1 344	92.7 192	85.5 186	46.2 91	55.9 581	62.5 451	68.1 266
Furs in sleeping [%] room of child n	2.0 101	2.5 316	3.9 179	7.9 164	0.0 88	2.3 558	3.1 426	2.0 255
Damp flat [%] n	5.0 120	7.8 345	3.7 189	3.7 188	19.2 94	15.5 601	12.5 458	7.3 273
Area of flat[m^2] n	86 119	91. 345	98 190	122 187	63 73	70 569	75 440	76 271
Persons /flat n	4.2 120	4.0 348	4.1 192	4.2 188	4.1 96	3.8 604	3.8 460	3.7 275

Lung function

Airway resistance showed no association to parental education, whereas the unadjusted ITGV were higher for children with better educated parents, as can be seen in Table 2. The regression coefficient was 18 ml/education class (s_b=7). This coefficient was reduced to a value of 9 (s_b=6), when height and birth weight were included in the model. Children with better educated parents had higher birth weights (Table 3) and were up to 2 cm higher (120 cm instead of 118 cm) than children of less well educated parents.

Immune reaction

The immunoglobulin and complement component concentrations in serum of the children did not vary with the educational level of the parents.

Allergological parameters

Questionnaire variables concerning irritation of the airways, infectious airway disease or bronchial asthma showed no association to educational status of the parents. Positive answers to allergy, hay fever, eczema, and ever wheezing, however, were more often given for children of better educated parents (Table 2). The odds ratio per education group was highest for hay fever (OR 3.7, CI_{95} 1.2 - 11.7). In West Germany dermatologists diagnosed atopic eczema at the day of the investigation about twice as often for children of the most educated parents than for those in the lowest education class (OR 1.8, CI_{95} 1.0 - 3.1). Positive concentrations of IgE antibodies against birch-, grass-, or mugwort pollen or against house dust or food allergens were found more often for children of better educated parents, too (OR 1.7, CI_{95} 1.2 - 2.4). Antibodies against mugwort pollen and grass pollen showed the highest single odds ratios (OR 2.3, CI_{95} 1.4-3.7). These associations were even stronger when the values from the small towns were excluded. In most cases the associations in East Germany were stronger than in West Germany.

51 variables were asked about in the questionnaire as possible confounders for the allergy-study, these were tested for their relation to education in order to find explanations for the strong association of allergy related variables with educational status. The eight variables showing the strongest association in either direction (4 positive 4 negative) are given with their frequencies in each educational class in Table 3.

In East Germany wall to wall carpets in the sleeping room of the child was more often present in the homes of better educated parents. In East as well as in West Germany better educated parents tended to bring furs in the sleeping room of the children more often, whereas the mean floor area of the homes of the more educated families was much larger in West Germany only. Those variables, characterizing the dwellings, where the children lived, were introduced into the logistic regression models in addition to educational status. Only the odds ratio between positive IgE antibodies against house dust mites and parental education was slightly reduced (OR: 1.5 to OR: 1.4) whereas all other odds ratios remained virtually unchanged.

The variables "smoking of mother in pregnancy", "low birth weight", "no breast-feeding" and "damp flat" could not explain the associations between allergy related variables and education of the parents at all. They were more often positive in the groups with lower educated parents. But non-adjusting for education led to positive associations between these variables and allergies. The odds ratio, for example, between "breast feeding > 8 weeks" and positive sensitization against grass pollen allergens changed from 1.08 to 0.99 after inclusion of education as a confounding factor.

46

DISCUSSION

Response

Before 1990 information about health effects of air pollution was not available in East Germany. This might be the reason for the higher response in East Germany than in West Germany. Main result of the study is that the associations between education and health parameters were strikingly similar in East and West Germany. There is no plausible mechanism, by which this similarity could be produced by differences in response rates.

Harmful substances in blood, teeth and urine

The association between blood lead and education of parents is well known and can be detected in most studies dealing with neurological impairments and lead [6]. The reason for that are less well understood. The fact, that children of lower social status tend to live in more polluted areas, is not the only explanation. In a study from 1983 we found that the regression coefficient between lead in dustfall and lead in blood was twice as high for children of lower social status than for the more privileged ones [7]. The difference in mean values between low social class children and high social class children living at the same place was larger when lead-concentrations in dustfall were higher. Different levels of hygiene may be responsible and could be discussed for this study, too.

Neurophysiological and neuropsychological variables

When comparing the influence of education and blood-lead on the results of the visual retention test it is clear that education is much more influential than lead. According to the regression analysis a change from 5 μg/dl to 10 μg/dl blood-lead would lead to a mean reduction in the visual retention test of only 0.2 point. Such a weak relationship is also true for other neuropsychological outcome variables. Social influences on children's neuropsychological development have usually been found to be more important than the influence of lead [6]. This stresses the necessity to adjust for these factors in a very careful manner since small residual confounding will lead to misleading results. The true underlying causality is likely to be complex.

Lung function

The association between measures of lung function and education of parents could nearly fully be explained by differences in height and birth weight of the children. Differences in height between members of different social classes are well documented [8]. They are among others causally related to dietary differences in early childhood. It is remarkable that those differences can be proven up to today. A recent study from Great Britain shows that even differences in birth weight are associated with differences in lung function in adult men [9].

Allergological parameters

Most studies dealing with the etiology of atopic diseases include some measurements of social factors as potential confounders [10]. Similar to our investigation bronchial asthma has not been related to social factors in most cases [11, 12]. Some studies have shown a higher asthma-prevalence for less privileged children [13]. The high number of positive answers to questions on hay-fever and eczema given by better educated parents is often interpreted as a detection bias [14]. Here it could be shown, however, that similar relations hold also for more objective measurements.

Sensitization rates and rates of diagnosed atopic eczema on the day of the investigation were higher for children of better educated parents. Similar associations have been found for prick tests and associations of social class with atopic eczema in other studies [15, 16]. The effect could not be explained by differences in the dwellings where the children live. The associations were strikingly similar in West and East Germany. Purely economic reasons can, therefore, not explain the relation. The number of siblings, which was shown to be negatively associated with hay-fever and sensitization rates [17, 18], also cannot explain this effect, because it does not differ too much across educational strata. The observed associations are similar to those in a just finished study in South Germany [19] and around the Baltic Sea [20]. Up to now the underlying cause is not understood. A more detailed investigation of the differences in child caretaking behavior between different social groups may help to clarify the etiology of these diseases.

SUMMARY

- Education of parents is an important influencing factor for most health outcome variables in children. Contrary to the well known fact that upper classes are healthier allergies are less frequent in the lower classes.

- Education has to be included as a confounding variable in the statistical analysis to prevent misleading interpretations. This has been shown for neuropsychological and allergological variables.

- As the education of parents cannot be a cause of a disease by itself, a striking association should always lead to a search for underlying causes. This has successfully been done for the lung function data and should be done for the allergological data, as well.

- The influence of parental education on the health outcome variables is even more pronounced in East than in West Germany. Purely economic reasons cannot lead to these differences.

ACKNOWLEDGEMENT

The study was partly supported by the Ministerium für Umwelt, Raumordnung und Landwirtschaft of Nordrhein-Westfalen and the Ministerium für Arbeit, Soziales und Gesundheit of Sachsen-Anhalt.

LITERATURE

1. Liberatos P, Link BG, Kelsey JL. The measurement of social class in epidemiology. *Epidemiologic Reviews* 1988;**10**:87-121.
2. Krämer U, Altus C, Behrendt H, Dolgner R, Gutsmuths FJ, Hille J, Hinrichs J, Mangold M, Paetz B, Ranft U, Röpke H, Teichmann S, Willer H-J, Schlipköter HW. Epidemiologische Untersuchungen zur Auswirkung der Luftverschmutzung auf die Gesundheit von Schulanfängern. *Forum Städte-Hygiene* 1992;**43**:82-87.
3. Winneke G, Altmann L, Krämer U, Turfeld M, Behler R, Gutsmuths FJ, Mangold M. Neurobehavioral and Neurophysiological Observations in Six Year Old Children with Low Lead Levels in East and West Germany. NeuroToxicology 1994;**15**:705-714.
4. Islam MS, Schlipköter HW. Lungenfunktion und Luftverunreinigung Der Bronchialtonus bei Kindern im Alter zwischen 6 und 9 Jahren in Gebieten mit unterschiedlichen Luftverunreinigungen. *Atemw Lungenkrankh* 1993;**19**:139-144.
5. Behrendt H, Krämer U, Dolgner R, Hinrichs J, Willer H, Hagenbeck H, Schlipköter HW. Elevated levels of total serum IgE in East German children: atopy, parasites, or pollutants? *Allergo J* 1993;**2**: 31-40.
6. Pocock SJ, Smith M, Baghurst P. Environmental lead and children's intelligence: a systematic review of the epidemiological evidence. *BMJ* 1994;**309**:1189-1197.
7. Krämer U. Methodische Aspekte in der Umweltepidemiologie, eds. H-E Wichmann. Medizinische Informatik und Statistik 65. Springer, Berlin, 1986.
8. Cernerud L. Growth and social conditions. The Nordic School of Public Health, Göteborg, 1991.
9. Strachan DP. Causes and control of chronic respiratory disease: looking beyond the smokescreen (Editorial). *J Epidemiol Community Health* 1992;**46**:177-179.
10. Ring J (eds). Epidemiologie allergischer Erkrankungen. MMV Medizin Verlag, München, 1991.

11. Burney PG. Asthma Epidemiology. *Br Med Bull* 1992;**48**:10-22.
12. Mitchell EA, Stewart AW, Pattemore PK, Asher MI, Marrison AC, Rea HH. Socioeconomic status in childhood asthma. *Int J Epidemiol* 1989;**18**:888-890.
13. Schwartz J, Gold D, Dockery DW, Weiss ST, Speizer FE. Predictors of asthma and persistent wheeze in a national sample of children in the United States. Associations with social class, perinatal events, and race. *Am Rev Respir Dis* 1990;**142**:555-562.
14. Sibbald B, Rink E. Labelling of rhinitis and hay fever by doctors. *Thorax* 1991;**46**:378-381.
15. Williams HC, Strachan DP, Hay RJ. Childhood eczema: disease of the advantaged? *BMJ* 1994;**308**: 1132-1135.
16. Gergen PJ, Turkellaub PC, Kovar MG. The prevalence of allergic skin test reactivity to eight common aeroallergens in the US population: Results from the second National Health and Nutrition Examination Survey. *J Allergy Clin Immunol* 1987;**80**:669-677.
17. Strachan DP. Hay fever, hygiene, and household size. *BMJ* 1989;**299**:1259-1260.
18. Mutius E, Fernando DM, Fritsch C, Nicolai T, Reitmeir P, Thiemann HH. Skin test reactivity and number of siblings. *BMJ* 1994;**308**:692-695.
19. Kuehr J, Frischer T, Karmans W, Menert R, Barth R, Urbanek R. Clinical atopy and associated factors in primary-school pupils. *Allergy* 1992;**47**:650-655.
20. Bråbäck L. Respiratory symptoms and atopic sensitization among school children in different settings around the Baltic Sea. Linköping University Medical Dissertations No 442. University Hospital, Linköping 1995.

INDUSTRIAL AIR POLLUTION IN A CONTEXT OF POVERTY: COMPARISON OF 27 LOCALITIES IN TWO BRITISH CITIES

Suzanne Moffatt[1], Peter Phillimore[2], Raj Bhopal[3], Christopher Foy[3], Christine Dunn[4]
[1]Departments of Epidemiology & Public Health and Social Policy, c/o The Medical School
The University, Newcastle upon Tyne NE2 4HH, UK.
[2] Department of Social Policy, Newcastle University
[3] Department of Epidemiology and Public Health, Newcastle University
[4] Department of Geography, Durham University

INTRODUCTION

Teesside, in northeast England, is home to one of Western Europe's largest petrochemical and steel complexes. During the early 1980s the area regularly suffered the highest unemployment rate in mainland Britain. The perceived problem of air pollution is experienced alongside acute problems of unemployment and consequent poverty in surrounding areas traditionally dependent on employment in local industry. Studies (1,2) have shown that many poorer parts of Teesside (made up chiefly of Middlesbrough and Stockton) had exceptionally high levels of premature mortality, far greater than would be expected taking account of deprivation levels. In fact a direct comparison of equally poor parts of Teesside and Sunderland, a city some 40 km north, showed that mortality was considerably lower in Sunderland. This led to a further study (3) which examined premature mortality in these two cities over a twelve year period (1975-1986). Throughout this period, death rates below the age of 65 years in Middlesbrough consistently exceeded death rates in comparable areas of Sunderland by a large margin (e.g. lung cancer standardised mortality ratios (SMRs) for men were 268 and 223 in Middlesbrough and Sunderland respectively; lung cancer SMRs for women were respectively 223 and 181). Most recently it has been shown that mortality in both these areas is worsening relative to the national picture, but that the gap in premature mortality between Teesside and Sunderland remains (4). It also emerged from this work that standardised illness ratios (SIRs) were relatively similar, 192 versus 188 in Middlesbrough and Sunderland respectively, in contrast to SMRs of 167 and 138 for the same areas.

Since records began, Teesside's health has been compared unfavourably with the rest of England and Wales (5). The Local Authority commissioned a health study in the early 1960s because of concern at high levels of mortality from lung cancer and bronchitis. More recently, concerns about health among the local Health Departments, health workers and residents have centred around possible links between air pollution from industry and ill-health.

This study has two main aims: first, to seek explanations for the persistent mortality differentials between Teesside and Sunderland and secondly, to examine whether industrial air pollution has an impact on the health of local populations in Teesside. This paper will outline the study design, which encompasses collection and linkage of social, economic, health and environmental data. In doing so, we aim to address four main issues:

i)   how we chose areas for study
ii) what health data we collected
iii) what environmental data we collected
iv) how we related health and environmental data

STUDY AREAS

Perhaps the most critical aspect of a study such as this is comparability of areas chosen for study. Our choice of areas was broadly based on previous research (1,2,3), although these studies were largely restricted to administrative areas known as wards, which are often not socially and economically homogeneous entities. To avoid the problem of working with these larger undifferentiated geographical units we evolved a procedure for selecting localities based upon the smallest geographical units for which Census data were available. These units (known as enumeration districts, which in urban areas consist of a number of streets with about 150 households) were then built up into larger areas with the same social and economic characteristics, usually corresponding to housing estates. In this study, we initially used social and economic information from the 1981 Census to identify enumeration districts. The major indicators were unemployment, car ownership, housing tenure and overcrowding from which an index summarising deprivation had been calculated (1,2). However, we also examined other social and economic indicators available from the Census, a further 14 in all, listed on Table 1 below. Following this initial selection we checked the evidence against primary field observations, examining how run-down areas appeared to be and how they compared with each other. Although inevitably superficial, it seemed to us it would be negligent to overlook direct observation in establishing our areas. Discussions about our choice of areas were held with Local Authority officers and local people. Finally, we used the newly available 1991 Census and examined social and economic indicators for each locality before finalising our choice. 27 comparable localities were finally selected, eight within Sunderland and nineteen within Teesside. The 27 localities were aggregated initially into four zones differing in proximity to industry on Teesside. Each locality was ascribed to a zone either near, intermediate or distant from industry (Zones A, B, C, respectively). Sunderland formed a separate fourth zone (Zone S). Subsequently different aggregations have been made to refine our comparison of areas.

Study areas of different size were adopted for different parts of the study for pragmatic reasons, being largest where routine statistics were available and smallest where original data collection was necessary. However, socioeconomic comparability was not compromised by varying the size of the study areas; different combinations of the various study localities did not substantially change the overall social and economic profile of the areas under scrutiny.

Thus far, choice of study areas rested almost exclusively on the use of Census data, which informed us about relative material deprivation. There has been considerable discussion about how well the four indicators used to construct the Townsend deprivation index reflect relative material hardship (2,6). However, information additional to economic and social indicators is necessary to ensure comparability in a detailed study of health status and is not available routinely. We therefore had to collect further data to the measurement of health status in different localities.

By means of a postal survey in 14 of the 27 localities, we obtained information about: housing conditions, working history and conditions, educational level, social support, access to health services, smoking, alcohol, exercise, dietary habits and perceived health status. This was done in a spread of localities across the four zones; a response rate of 62% yielded a sample size of 6,377. The survey data enabled us to go a step further than previous studies (1,2,3,4) by allowing us to examine whether these mortality differentials might be partially or wholly explained by differences in housing conditions, access to health services, working history and conditions, social support or health related behaviour. Table 2, below, shows how similar the areas proved to be; in fact employment history was the only factor that differed significantly between the zones. Social and economic information is also incorporated into the analysis of health status allowing us to account for any differences observed.

Table 1.   1981 Census Indicators examined at enumeration district level

*Unemployment	Single parent head of household
Male unemployment	Children in single parent families
Female unemployment	Lone pensioners
Unemployed 16-24 year olds	Migrants
*Households with no car	Local Authority rented house
*Owner occupied households	Residents not in private households
*Over crowded households	Households with shared bathroom & WC
17 year olds in full-time education	Households with no children
Single parent households	Head of household born in
	New Commonwealth/Pakistan

----

* Main indicators used for comparison

HEALTH DATA

A range of data was collected with the aim of allowing us to examine mortality and morbidity, the latter both from doctors' records and self-reports. Routinely available data - mortality, cancer registration, stillbirths, low birthweight babies and foetal abnormalities - were obtained for an 11 year period in all 27 localities in the four zones. Patterns of mortality for birth cohorts from 1921 can be examined, but in only two of the four zones (Middlesbrough and Sunderland). This will provide an indication of the pattern of deaths spanning almost a century.

Specially collected data were, of necessity, obtained for a smaller number of localities. Information on self-reported chronic ill-health, illnesses and recent symptoms was gathered from an age-sex stratified sample (N= 6,377) within 14 localities. A smaller sample (N=2,194) linked with the survey informants was drawn from 8 localities in the three Teesside Zones to acquire morbidity data recorded by general practitioners. In this part of the study, data concerning daily consultations (date, diagnosis/symptom), hospital admissions, repeat prescriptions and chronic conditions were extracted from patient records for a 5 year period ending September 1994. Taken as a whole, this data-set allowed us to investigate patterns of ill-health from the most to arguably the least severe, both chronic and acute and based upon routinely available statistics, doctors' notes and informants' replies.

There were several grounds for not wishing to rely on one type of health data to inform us about levels of ill-health in the populations studied. First, because reliance on a single health data-set would limit the picture of ill-health within the community to a single dimension.   Second, because a range of data allows comparison between health datasets for consistency and plausibility of any health effect observed; for example, mortality and morbidity, although closely related, are often not identical (4). Thirdly, data linkage, for instance in our study, between self-reported ill-health and general practitioners' records allows validation of self-reports for certain medically confirmable conditions and allows examination of reporting bias. Concerns over sensitised populations need to be addressed, particularly when self-reported data are used. A range of health data does help to examine this issue, as a more detailed profile of ill-health can be built up and checks on the pattern of responses to questions in the context of other health evidence can be made. This issue is extremely complex, particularly in environmental epidemiological studies, and we have attempted to address it in more depth elsewhere (7).

Table 2.   Comparison of study zones on selected variables

	Zone A N=19,925 %	Zone B N=34,753 %	Zone C N=22,652 %	Zone S N=42,681 %
1991 Census data				
Unemployment	32	31	33	29
Households with no car	68	73	70	72
Persons in overcrowded households	9	8	9	7
Owner occupied households	25	27	20	21
1993 Survey Data	**N=1,539**	**N=1,464**	**N=1,486**	**N=1910**
Current smokers	40	42	42	37
Alcohol consumed on most days	12	10	10	9
Take exercise most days	11	10	10	12
Left school 16 years or under	93	94	94	94
Damp housing	3	2	2	3
Employment for more than 1 year in:				
- steel/iron industry	48	43	28	7
- coal mining industry	2	2	2	10
- chemical industry	21	18	17	3

ENVIRONMENTAL DATA

For environmental data we were reliant upon that already collected by the Local Authority. The study spanned a period in which a comprehensive national black smoke and sulphur dioxide (SO_2) monitoring network was being run down. It was replaced by a much smaller number of more technologically advanced sites monitoring SO_2, oxides of nitrogen (NOx), and one site monitoring particulate matter less than 10 μm in diameter (PM_{10}) and volatile organic compounds (VOCs).

We do know, however, from the national network that Middlesbrough had amongst the highest levels of smoke and SO_2 in Britain during the 1960s (8). Throughout that decade there was a steady downward trend in pollution levels. Although this was also observed in Middlesbrough, levels of smoke and SO_2 in one of our localities, sited close to a steel and coking works, lagged behind this national trend and remained steady until the 1970s (8). The more recent monitored data we have access to are daily and continuous and of a much higher quality than that obtained via the old national monitoring network. However, such technological refinement in the range of pollutants measured, the accuracy of measurement and the level of time disaggregation has one major drawback: a loss in spatial coverage within a city.

Because of the small number of sites, a pilot monitoring study was undertaken in all study areas to measure benzene, toluene and xylene. This pilot study has provided us with the only comparable environmental dataset for the four study zones.

A third data source has been industrial emissions data from the major industries in the area. These data are to be used in a pollution modelling exercise to examine the pattern of emission dispersion in relation to the localities chosen for the health study.

Finally, a historical land use survey was carried out in the three Teesside zones detailing industrial land usage between 1900 and 1994. The particular industrial history of Middlesbrough, involving rapid expansion of iron, steel, railways, shipbuilding and latterly chemical industries from the 1860s coupled with much older and well-established industry in the Stockton area made it advisable to check the past land use of areas currently occupied by housing. The study localities in Sunderland were distant from local industry, which centred around shipbuilding and mining, and it was not necessary to undertake a detailed land use survey in this area.

INTEGRATING HEALTH AND ENVIRONMENTAL DATA

The initial analysis of all the health data is based on proximity of each locality to industry. In addition to proximity to the source, we have sought to 'measure' exposure status by means of all the data at our disposal, which in this case includes exposure based on modelled emissions and actual environmental measurements. The highly complex nature of assessing exposure to pollution mitigates against reliance on a single measure, just as we would avoid a single measurement of health or socioeconomic status. We will therefore examine a range of exposure measurements in parallel with a range of health measurements. This process of relating health and environmental data is crucial to addressing questions about ill-health and pollution. Our approach is twofold: integrating health and environmental datasets in space and in time.

(i) Spatial data linkage

An alternative spatial grouping of study localities may be derived from the model of industrial emissions. The routine health data, covering all the study areas, can easily be re-classified into new exposure categories using contoured pollutant values in a geographical information system (GIS) and subsequently reanalysed. The exercise can be repeated for each pollutant used in the model (in this case, carbon monoxide, oxides of nitrogen, benzene, toluene and xylene). In a recent study, investigating the health effects from coking plant emissions (9) mortality and cancer registration data were reanalysed based on modelled SO_2. In that study areal definition based on proximity and SO_2 emissions proved to be similar and no differences were found between the analyses. Modelling provides a basis for linking health and environmental data in space, but it does have considerable limitations. For instance, input data are based on stack emissions and exclude low level or fugitive emissions, which may have greater impact on pollution levels in areas close to the industry. It was not possible to obtain data from every industrial site, as, although invited, not all industries agreed to submit data. Furthermore, modelling on this scale, using yearly averaged emissions data, inevitably irons out variations, making it impossible to pick up health effects of short-term peaks. Mortality, cancer registration and birth data, rather than acute episodes of ill-health, are linked in this case.

(ii) Temporal data linkage

Exploration of links between short-term variation in pollution levels and ill-health is possible because of accurate dating of both GP records and daily pollution monitoring. Specifically, we will link the date and diagnosis of each consultation with levels of PM_{10}, SO_2 and NO_2. Analysis will take account of temperature, wind direction, season and day of the week. In comparing GP consultations with pollution levels on the same day, we are assuming that any health effects are likely to be observable rapidly. However, the analysis will investigate possible time-lag effects found in other studies of routine data and air quality (10,11). Because monitoring was carried out in only two of the three Teesside localities, leaving no environmental data for analysis with the 'least exposed' group, limitations are placed on our conclusions. However, we hope to be able to identify any relationship, which may exist between short-term variations in pollution levels and episodes of ill-health in the highest and intermediate exposure groups.

We intend to link two health and two environmental datasets. The historical land use survey and pilot monitoring study provide extremely useful background information about the areas chosen.

SUMMARY

In seeking to answer questions about industrial pollution and ill-health, it is necessary to first measure socioeconomic, health and exposure status, then to integrate the datasets. Capturing each of these parameters accurately is a difficult matter. We have attempted to examine a range of factors that together, describe socioeconomic, health and exposure status.

Central to our study design was choice of area, based on location in relation to industry and socioeconomic characteristics. Using both Census data and specially collected survey data, we have demonstrated that the 27 localities in the study were well matched on a range of social, economic and health-related factors. We identified major differences which would influence health: in this case occupation in heavy industry and exposure to hazards at work. The results are not surprising, given the different industrial histories of Teesside and Sunderland. Within our limited time and resources, collecting more detail on all possible social, economic and health-related factors, which may have a bearing on health, would have been impossible. We believe it is unlikely that we have missed a potentially major influence on health, which differs in these localities, and that we have fairly reflected the socioeconomic conditions of those in our study.

Health status is arguably more difficult to assess. Although we relied on more than a single measure, we were unable to undertake new data collection in every one of the twenty-seven localities. Furthermore, for practical reasons it was not possible to collect GP morbidity data in Sunderland, thereby removing the scope for comparison of these data outside Teesside.

However, it seems to us that in a study such as this, exposure status is the most problematical to assess. There are no comparable data across the study areas, unlike Census data or routine health statistics. Considerable gaps existed in coverage of the areas under study: air quality monitoring was available in two out of the four study zones; emissions data were not available from all industrial sites on Teesside; and we have no information about actual individual exposure.

In spite of the difficulties imposed by gaps in the measurement of health and exposure status, we will be able to integrate certain health and exposure measurements. In doing so, we aim to draw conclusions within the limitations imposed by our data, about the impact of industrial pollution on health. ([#]

ACKNOWLEDGEMENTS

In addition to the authors, this work is being carried out by Ms Jacqui Tate of Newcastle University; Dr John Edwards of Flinders University, South Australia; Dr Jim Longstaff , Ms Jo Denn and Ms Lesley Sharpe of Teesside University; Dr Erasmus Harland and Dr Ian Holtby of Tees Health, Mrs Catherine Hall of Langbaurgh Borough Council and Mr Jeff Duffield of Middlesbrough Borough Council. We gratefully acknowledge financial support from Cleveland Family Health Serices Authority, Tees Health, Middlesbrough City Challenge, The Northern and Yorkshire Regional Health Authority and Cleveland County Council.

REFERENCES

1. Townsend P, Phillimore P, Beattie A. Inequalities in Health in the Northern Region. An Interim Report. A Report to Northern Regional Health Authority and University of Bristol, 1986.
2. Townsend P, Phillimore P, Beattie A. Health and Deprivation. Inequality and the North. Croom Helm, London, 1988.
3. Phillimore P. and Morris D. Discrepant Lagacies: Premature Mortality in Two Industrial Towns. *Soc. Sci. Med.* 1991; **33**: 139-152.
4. Phillimore P. and Beattie A. Health and Inequality. The Northern Region 1981-1991. A report published by the Department of Social Policy, University of Newcastle upon Tyne, 1994.
5. Nicholas, K. The social effects of unemployment on Teesside. Manchester University Press, Manchester, 1986.
6. Townsend P. Poverty in the United Kingdom. Penguin, Harmondsworth, Middlesex, 1979.
7. Moffatt S. Phillimore P, Bhopal R, Foy C. "If this is what it's doing to our washing, what is it doing to our lungs?" Public understanding and industrial pollution in north-east England. *Soc. Sci. Med.* 1995,41,6,883-891.
8. Dean G, Lee PN, Todd GF, Wicken AJ. Report on a second retrospective mortality study in North-East England. Part II: Changes in lung cancer and bronchitis mortality and in other relevant factors occurring in areas of North-East England 1963-72. Tobacco Research Council Research Paper 14, 1977.
9. Bhopal R, Phillimore P, Moffatt S, Foy C. Is living near a coking works harmful to health? A study of industrial air pollution. *Jnl Epid & Comm Hlth.* 1994; **48**: 237-247.
10. Walters S, Griffiths R, Ayres J. Air pollution and acute respiratory disease: a study using routinely collected data. Unpublished paper presented at the National Public Health Conference, W.Midlands Regional Health Authority, 1991.
11. Mackenbach JP, Looman CWN, Kunst AE. Air pollution, lagged effects of temperature, and mortality: The Netherlands 1979-87. *Jnl Epid & Comm Hlth.* 1993, 47: 121-126.

[#]) The study was completed in december 1995. A full account of the background, methods and results are available in a 400 page report entitled *Health, Illness and the Environment in Teesside and Sunderland*, ISBN No. 0-7017-0064-5. Available from Dr. Suzanne Moffatt / Dept. of Epidemiology and Public Health / The University of Newcastle / Newcastle Upon Tyne, NE2 4HH / U.K.

Subjective and Objective Indicators of Air Pollution, Education, Lifestyle and Respiratory Health

Peter Lercher, Rudolf Schmitzberger
University of Innsbruck, Sonnenburgstraße 16, A-6020 Innsbruck, Austria

SUMMARY

The relationship between traffic air pollution, education and several indices of respiratory health was studied among schoolchildren (aged 8-12) in a cross-sectional study (N = 796, 85% response) of 13 small alpine communities (Tyrol/Austria). Individual exposure assignment was based on NO_2 (14-28 $\mu g/m^3$) exposure and subjective rating of perceived air quality (child's mother). Respiratory health was assessed by a standardized illness questionnaire and flow volume curves.

None of the respiratory illnesses was significantly associated with NO_2 or educational level. However, there was a strong trend for dichotomized indicators of small airways impairment ($MEF_{50} < 70\%$, $MEF_{75} < 70\%$) to be inversely associated with educational achievement. Regression analysis of standardized continuous flow curves revealed significant mean differences for higher educational attainment with all indices (23-77 ml). Neither 'subjective' nor 'objective' indicators of air pollution did show a consistent or significant relation with any of the lung function measures. However, high altitude (> 1100m) and low birthweight (< 2500g) were negatively associated with the flow curves and low birthweight did show a marked interaction with educational level: only the lower educational stratum (< 9 years of education) was affected by the negative impact of low birthweight.

INTRODUCTION

Birth cohort studies in the UK have shown that social differences in health exist already early in life and still contribute towards health differentials later in life (1, 2). Inheritance at birth, education, life style and behaviour, environmental and socioeconomic circumstances are believed to interrelate in a complex manner not yet fully understood (2). There is further evidence for differential awareness of air pollution and associated health risks due to education, socioeconomic and cultural factors (3). However, it has not yet sufficiently been studied whether subjective perceptions and appraisals act as potential moderators towards health effects or contribute only to exposure misclassification (4). Therefore, in a recent field study on the asserted health impact of low level road traffic air pollution on children in the Alpine area of Tyrol an integrative approach was applied. In addition to 'objective' measures of air pollution also 'subjective' indicators of perceived air quality were included.

This complementary approach was based on the notion that some effects of environmental exposures may be triggered or mediated by perception or by the consequences of coping with the experienced exposures (3, 4). In this area traffic volume has quadrupled over the past twenty years while non-traffic air pollution (SO_2) has been substantially reduced.

It is the main aim of this paper to study whether road traffic air pollution in rural areas is currently affecting selected measures of respiratory health in schoolchildren.

Secondly we wanted to analyse whether the supposed effect in children of parents with different educational background varies and whether subjective ratings of perceived air pollution are playing a mediating role

METHODS

Study population and sites: Second, third and fourth grade schoolchildren (aged 7.5-12, N=796, 85% overall participation) were recruited from 7 'exposed' communities with traffic density over 10 000 vehicles/day. Participation with lung function testing was slightly lower (N=744). The study sites were situated along major traffic arteries and selected after careful exclusion of communities with moderate SO_2/SPM exposure or other relevant sources of pollution than road traffic. A dominating feature was a high proportion of heavy trucks (3 500-5 500/day). The 6 'unexposed' communities were chosen from adjacent areas and their predominantly local traffic did not exceed 5 000 vehicles/day. The altitude of the study sites varies from 500 up to 1350 m. Topographically, 'exposed' sites are situated in larger valleys while the 'unexposed' sites are situated in more mountainous and narrower valleys. Because residential mobility of this area is very low and > 90% of the children have lived in their village since birth, the occurrence of selection factors of this kind is unlikely.

Exposure assessment: Basic data on air pollutants (SO_2, NO_2, O_3) were available from nearby monitoring sites. Additional measurements (Palmes tubes, mobile bus, special studies) were conducted to supplement and to evaluate exposure estimates provided by the head of the regional air pollution unit. Exposure assignments of schoolchildren were based on NO_2 as indicator pollutant at their home address. Table 1 gives a short summary of the air pollution experience in this area. It shows that the 'exposed' area differs distinctly only by NO_2 and Benzopyrene levels of exposure. Furthermore, WHO Air Quality Guidelines (1987) were not exceeded. Subjective perceptions of traffic exhaust fumes were rated by the child's mother on a 5 grade scale (never perceptible to always perceptible).

Confounder and Mediator assessment: A standardized mother completed questionnaire revealed broad information on the child's predispositions, the home environment (room, heating, pets, smoking), and parental predispositions, education, area of work. Education was assessed according to the Central Bureau of Statistics, based on the number of years in school. For the purpose of this study the mothers' educational status was used and dichotomized ($\geq$ or < 9 years of education).

Health assessment: Asthma, acute and chronic bronchitis, eczema were assessed by questionnaire based on doctors' diagnoses ('Has your child ever had ...'). Hayfever was assessed by a question on symptoms during the current year. 'Wheezing' was evaluated by a short questionnaire (5) and dichotomized based on a score (> 3 points). Flow volume curves were obtained by a computerized pneumotachograph (Multi Spiro PC). The associated software displayed a birthday cake with burning candles on the screen and assured excellent cooperation (the stronger the expiration the easier to blow out the candles). During the test each child was sitting and wearing a nose clip. The testing standards of the American Thoracic Society were applied. Two trained physicians performed the measurements after the daily calibration of the spirometer. Anthropometrics (body weight, length, blood pressure) were obtained on the same day.

Statistical analysis: Multiple logistic regression was used to estimate the independent effect of education and the other predictors on respiratory illnesses. The relative contributions were estimated by Wald scores. A best model strategy was applied based on a flexible backwards elimination strategy.

Each index of pulmonary function was analysed separately by multiple linear regression methods. Predictors were checked for their additional contribution. Raw and standardized values were evaluated. Standardization (age, length, weight) was performed separately for each sex based on the regression formulas of Neuberger *et al.* (6). Possible interactions were evaluated by graphical means (coplots). SAS 6.08 and S-PLUS 3.2 for Windows were used. Several macros from F. Harrell helped making diagnostic plots and by-variable analyses.

Table 1.   Air pollution characteristic of study sites

Air Pollutant	Exposed (*	Controls (*	WHO-AQG
SO_2	8 - 25 $\mu g/m^3$	7 - 24 $\mu g/m^3$	50 $\mu g/m^3$ (†
NO_2	14 - 28 $\mu g/m^3$	4 - 10 $\mu g/m^3$	60 $\mu g/m^3$ (†
O_3 (#	140 - 180 $\mu g/m^3$	140 - 200 $\mu g/m^3$	200 $\mu g/m^3$ (✿
SPM	25 - 45 $\mu g/m^3$	15 - 30 $\mu g/m^3$	60 $\mu g/m^3$ (†
B(a)P	> 0.2 ng/m^3	< 0.2 ng/m^3	NA

*) Ranges in the communities   ✿)1 hour upper limit
#) Half hour peaks   †) 1 year limit

RESULTS

Despite one small village with a markedly lower proportion of mothers with higher education, there was no significant difference between 'exposed' and 'unexposed' communities with respect to educational level. Among the potential confounder and effect modifiers (Table 2) we see a bunch of variables showing relevant crude associations ($p < 0.1$) with the educational attainment of the child's mother. However, none of the respiratory illnesses (Table 3) show a significant association with educational level.

An earlier analysis (7) has demonstrated significant associations of chronic bronchitis, recurrent colds, and hyperresponsiveness with a subjective indicator of air quality (frequency of perceived traffic fumes), but failed to show accompanying links with a dichotomized index of NO_2 exposure. The current analysis did not provide any hint for an interaction effect between educational level and subjective rating of air quality.

Evaluation of several dichotomized indicators of relevant lung function impairment (Table 4) revealed a marked prevalence of reduction with the Maximal Expiratory Flow at 75% of Vital Capacity expired. Furthermore, this condition was significantly inversely associated with educational achievement. A similar trend with education can already be seen at 50% expired (MEF_{50}) which adds credence to the observed result at MEF_{75}.

Moreover, only a very small fraction is added to the total variance explained by the basic standardized model (up to 5%) through the addition of educational attainment or any other significant variable. Neither 'subjective' nor 'objective' indicators of air pollution did show a consistent or significant relation with any of the lung function measures.

Table 2. Potential confounder/effect modifier associated with higher educational level of child's mother (≥ 9 years).

Variable groups	Crude odds ratio	95 % Confidence Interval
Dispositions		
Preterm birth (< 37 weeks)	0.61	0.42 to 0.89
First birth	1.51	1.12 to 2.03
General environment		
Altitude > 1100 m	0.54	0.33 to 0.86
Mother involved in farming	0.62	0.36 to 1.06
Adjacent highway/main road	1.35	0.97 to 1.88
NO2 exposure > 20 $\mu g/m^3$	1.47	1.08 to 2.01
Home environment		
> 4 persons/family	0.70	0.52 to 0.94
< 90 m^3 living space	0.60	0.40 to 0.88
Single room heating	0.69	0.49 to 0.99
Carpeted floor	0.73	0.51 to 1.03
Behaviour		
Nonsmoking household	1.64	1.20 to 2.23
Outdoor activities > 4 hrs (winter	0.53	0.33 to 0.86
Outdoor activities > 4 hrs (summer	0.61	0.40 to 0.92

Table 3. Respiratory illness and adjusted odds ratios associated with higher educational level of child's mother (≥ 9 years).

Condition	Prevalence (%)	Odds ratio (*	95 % Confidence Interval
Acute bronchitis	10.0	1.17	0.70 to 1.96
Chronic bronchitis	3.8	0.87	0.36 to 2.12
Asthma bronchiale	4.0	0.97	0.39 to 2.44
Hayfever	9.2	0.88	0.51 to 1.54
Recurrent colds	9.7	1.35	0.79 to 2.29
Hyperresponsive (#	4.5	1.01	0.45 to 2.25

*) Adjusted for several dispositional and environmental variables by logistic regression
#) Index from seven asthma specific questions (score >3 points)

Table 4. Lung function impairment and associated odds ratios with higher educational level of child's mother (≥ 9 years).

Condition	Prevalence (%)	Odds ratio (*	95 % Confidence Interval
FVC < 80 %	1.1	na	na
FEV1 < 80 %	2.0	0.87	0.29 to 2.61
PEF < 80 %	3.1	0.88	0.36 to 2.14
MEF25 < 80 %	4.6	1.30	0.62 to 2.70
MEF50 < 70 %	6.3	0.61	0.30 to 1.21
MEF75 < 70 %	21.1	0.59	0.39 to 0.89

*) Adjusted for several dispositional and environmental variables by logistic regression

Regression analysis of continuous lung function measurements (Table 5) revealed significant mean differences for educational status with all indices. However, the estimated effect size is rather small and does not follow the pattern we have observed with the dichotomized lung function indices, showing an increasing effect the more volume is expired.

Table 5. Size (* of raw, partially adjusted, and standardized lung function coefficients associated with higher educational level of child's mother (≥ 9 years).

Lung Function	Raw mean differences (95 % CI)	Length adjusted mean differences (95 % CI)	Standardized (# mean differences (95 % CI)
FVC	82(31 to 133)	38(0 to 77)	58(17 to 99)
FEV1	95(36 to 153)	35(-1 to 72)	49(14 to 83)
PEF1	54(18 to 292)	63(-53 to 178)	77(14 to 140)
MEF25	125(-9 to 258)	52(-67 to 170)	71(19 to 123)
MEF50	117(11 to 222)	76(-25 to 176	49(13 to 84)
MEF75	31(-3 to 89)	12(-45 to 70)	23(6 to 41)

*) in ml
#) Age, length, weight, and sex standardized after Neuberger et al. 1993

DISCUSSION

The results of this study suggest that educational attainment of the mother is significantly associated with lung function measures in this area. Children of mothers with fewer years of education show consistently lower lung function values. However, the relative impact is small and an additional entry of education to the already standardized regression model did not contribute much to the explained variance. When we consider the other predictors, neither air pollution indices nor other home environment variables were significantly associated with lung function. From the rest of the variables low birthweight and high altitude (> 1100 m) were consistently associated with all the indices of lung function (negative impact). While the effect of altitude ranges within the size observed with education, low birth exhibits a three times larger estimated effect than education. Nevertheless, its additional contribution to the total variance explained is as small as with altitude or education. This fact triggered some further analyses.

Since altitude and preterm birth (highly linked with low birthweight) were associated with education (Table 2), we considered evaluating possible interaction of these factors with education. Figure 1 and Figure 2 show the results of the interaction plots. Education and low birthweight exhibit a marked interaction: The negative impact of low birthweigth is evident only among those mothers with less than 9 years of education. No unfavourable effect can be seen among the mothers with higher education. It seems that this strong interaction is masking part of the real effect. When you visually inspect the estimated effect on the y-axis you can see that the mean difference for the lung function indices among the lower educated is much larger than the estimated size for education in Table 5. On the other hand, altitude shows a consistent small effect on lung function. The true underlying cause is currently subject of speculation (8, 9).

Another methodological consideration is concerned with traditional strategies of adjustment in regression modelling. E.g. body length is such a strong determinant of lung function that no study can omit adjustment to this factor. However, in the light of a significant relationship of education with body length [1.4 (0.50 to 2.31) cm in this study], most of the assumed effect of education may already have been accounted for by standardization for length. This is important because 1 cm of body length is already associated with a larger impact on lung function than the estimated impact for education from Table 5.

Therefore, the general practice may lead to an underestimation of the true effect size of educational level and 'biologize' social facts. This potential methodological pitfall has already been mentioned by other authors who were concerned with smoking (10). A recent editorial (11) has pointed out to look 'beyond the smokescreen', to consider SES and to evaluate 'the extent to which such socioeconomic gradients reflect upbringing and living conditions in childhood'. This may also concern some results of recent studies, linking traffic air pollution to respiratory health (12, 13, 14, 15, 16). Since living near busy urban roads is often associated with lower socioeconomic status (not in our study with rural sites), it seems very important to consider SES adequately in these studies.

CONCLUSIONS

Air pollution epidemiology should not view indices of socioeconomic status as mere confounders. To reveal the real factors behind the observed social class gradients it is recommended to screen more rigorously for potential interactions. This seems especially important in air pollution studies, because socioeconomic circumstances are often associated both with air pollution exposure (e.g. traffic, industry) and with powerful predictors of respiratory outcomes (e.g. low birthweight, nutrition). Furthermore, standard strategies of adjustment in regression modelling may result in overfitting of the model and therefore underestimate the true effect of socioeconomic factors on health.

REFERENCES

1. Blaxter M. The health of children: Studies in deprivation and disadvantage. Heinemann, London, 1981.
2. Power C, Manor O, Fox J. Health and class: The early years. Chapman & Hill, London, 1991.
3. Evans GW, Jacobs SV. Air pollution and human behavior. In: Environmental stress (Evans GW, ed.), Cambridge University Press, New York, 1982: 105-132.
4. Evans GW. The psychological costs of chronic exposure to ambient air pollution. In: The vulnerable brain and environmental risks, Vol 3 (Isaacson RL, Jensen KF, eds), Plenum Press, New York, 1994: 167-182.
5. Kühr J, Hendel-Kramer A, Stephan V, Karmaus W, Urbanek R. Epidemiologische Erfassung von Asthma bronchiale beim Schulkind. *Pneumologie* 1989; **43**: 703-709.
6. Neuberger M, Wiesenberger W, Kundi M, Zidek Th. Fluß-Volumen-Referenzwerte für Pflichtschüler. *Atemw.-Lungenkrkh* 1993; **19**: S87-S90.
7. Lercher P, Schmitzberger R, Kofler W. Perceived traffic air pollution, associated behavior and health in an alpine area. *Sci Total Environ* 1995; **169**: 71-74.
8. Schmitzberger R, Rhomberg K, Kemmler G. Chronic exposure to ozone and respiratory health of children. *Lancet* 1992; **339**: 881-882.
9. Schmitzberger R, Rhomberg K, Büchele H, Puchegger R, Schmitzberger-Natzmer D, Kemmler G, Panosch B. Effects of air pollution on the respiratory tract of children. *Pediatr Pulmonol* 1983; **15**: 68-74.
10. Jarvis MJ, Strachan DP, Feyerabend C. Determinants of passive smoking in children in Edinburgh, Scotland. *Am J Public Health* 1992; **82**:1225-1229.
11. Strachan DP. Causes and control of chronic respiratory disease: looking beyond the smokescreen. J *Epidemiol Community Health* 1992; **46**: 177-179.
12. Clench-Aas J, Larssen S, Bartonova A, Aarnes MJ, Myhre K, Christensen CC, Neslein IL, Thomassen Y, Levy F. The health effects of traffic pollution as measured in the Vålerenga area of Oslo. NILU, Lillestrœm, Norway, 1991.
13. Nitta H, Sato T, Nakai S, Maeda K, Aoki S, Ono M. Respiratory health associated with exposure to automobile exhaust. I. Results of Cross-sectional studies in 1979, 1982, and 1983. *Arch Environ Health* 1993; **48**: 53-58.
14. Wjst M, Reitmeir P, Dold S, Wulff A, Nicolai Th, Loeffelholz-Colberg E, Mutius E. Road traffic and adverse effects on respiratory health in children. *BMJ* 1993; **307**: 596-600.
15. Weiland SK, Mundt KA, Rückmann A, Keil U. Self-reported wheezing and allergic rhinitis in children and traffic density on street of residence. *AEP* 1994; **4**:243-247.
16. Edwards J, Walters S, Griffiths RK. Hospital admissions for asthma in preschool children: relationship to major roads in Birmingham, United Kingdom. *Arch Environ Health* 1994; **49**: 223-227.

Fig. 1. Standardized lung functions, education, and low birthweight

(Adjusted for age, body length, body weight, and gender)

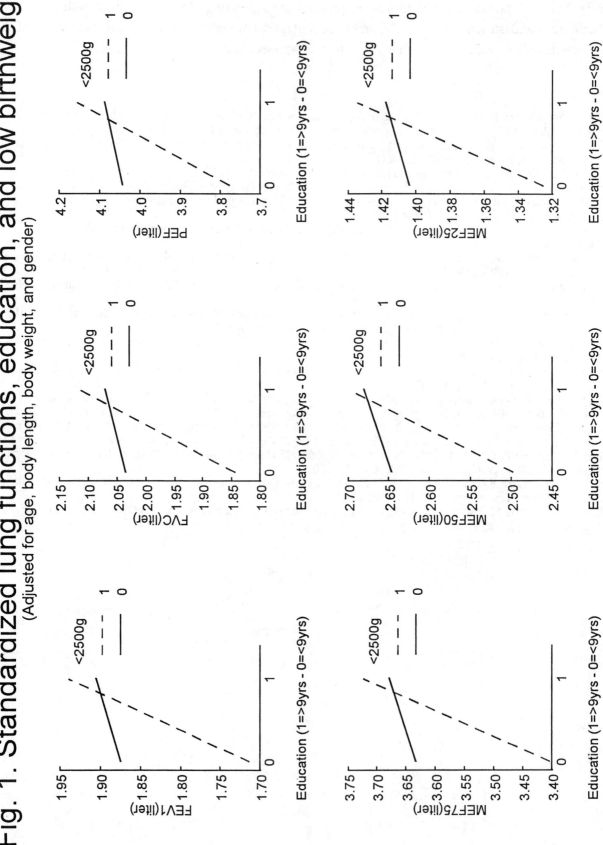

Fig. 2. Standardized lung functions, education, and altitude >1100m
(Adjusted for age, body length, body weight, and gender)

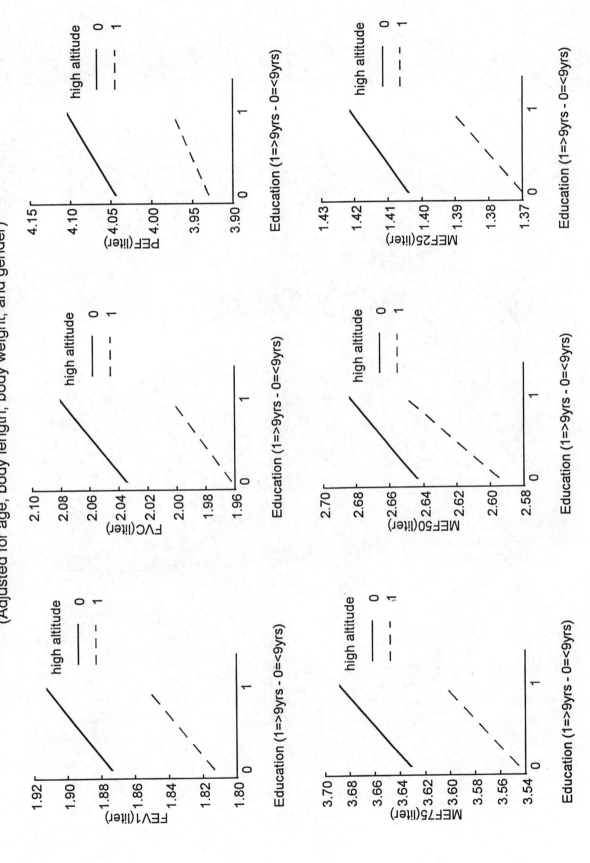

EFFECTS OF AIR POLLUTANTS AND SOCIOECONOMIC FACTORS ON NEUROBEHAVIORAL PERFORMANCE IN CZECH SCHOOL CHILDREN

I. Skalík[1], D. Otto[2], R. Šrám[1], D. Dvořáková[1], J. Tse[3]

[1]Regional Institute of Hygiene of Central Bohemia. Dittrichova 17, Prague 2, 12000, CZECH
[2]NHEERL, U.S. Environmental Protection Agency. Research Triangle Park, NC 27511,USA
[3]School of Public Health, University of North Carolina. Chapel Hill, NC 27514, USA

SUMMARY

Neurobehavioral performance was assessed in large cohorts of 2nd, 4th and 8th grade children living in districts of Bohemia with varying levels of air pollution. A questionnaire was used to obtain demographic, socioeconomic and health history data from parents to assess the possible confounding effects of these variables. District differences in performance were observed in 2nd and 8th grade cohorts, but similar differences in the 4th grade cohort disappeared when scores were adjusted for parental education and other possible confounders. Results demonstrate the importance of controlling for socioeconomic and demographic covariates in environmental neuroepidemiology.

INTRODUCTION

Research on the adverse health effects of chemical exposure in human populations has grown exponentially during the past 25 years. Environmental health effect studies usually focus on the measurement of chemical exposure in the ambient air, biomarkers of exposure, and physiological measures of organ function - e.g. spirometric measurement of forced vital capacity. However, health effect measures can also be influenced subtly (or dramatically) by sociocultural factors such as ethnicity, education, occupation, income, type of housing, family structure and size. These factors can mask or amplify health effects associated with pollutant exposure and, therefore, must be controlled in the design or analysis of data from health effects studies. Too often such factors are ignored or poorly controlled, seriously compromising the interpretation of results. Neurobehavioral measures of sensorimotor and cognitive function are particularly susceptible to the influence of sociocultural factors (1). A series of studies of neurobehavioral function in Czech school children has been conducted during the past few years in conjunction with the Teplice Programme. The basic objective of these studies was to compare the neurobehavioral performance of children living in districts of Bohemia with varying levels of air pollution. Results of these studies and efforts to control for the possible confounding of sociocultural factors will be reviewed below.

METHODS

Study area.

Northern Bohemia is one of the most polluted areas in Europe (2). High levels of sulphur dioxide, nitrogen oxides, polycyclic aromatic hydrocarbons and heavy metals occur as a result of intensive mining and combustion of brown coal for power generation and heating, topographic features of the environment, and frequent temperature inversions during winter. Although many of these pollutants are not generally associated with neurobehavioral deficits,

Gebhart *et al.* (3), suggested that children living in the polluted region may be at greater risk for minimal brain dysfunction than other children in the Czech Republic. Šrám (2) hypothesized that *in utero* exposure to these chemicals causes functional changes in the nervous system expressed as developmental disorders, attention-deficit disorders or other behavioural dysfunctions. Many trace metals including arsenic (As), mercury (Hg) and cadmium (Cd) occur as byproducts of the combustion of brown coal (4). Exposure to one or more of these heavy metals could produce neurotoxicity in humans (5). Children are known to be particularly susceptible to methylmercury poisoning (6).

The heavily polluted mining district of Teplice in Northern Bohemia was chosen for health effect studies. The agricultural district of Prachatice in Southern Bohemia was chosen for control purposes. No coal mines or power plants are located in the Prachatice District. Ambient levels of selected air pollutants in the two districts during peak winter exposure months are shown in Table 1. Pollutant levels are substantially higher in the Teplice district. Since brown coal is burned for heating in some homes in ·Prachatice, a third district - Znojmo, which uses natural gas for power and heating - was added recently as a second control area.

Table 1. **Ambient Air Levels of Selected Air Pollutants in Teplice and Prachatice during the Winter (January - March) of 1993**

Species	Teplice	Prachatice
SO_2 ($\mu g/m^3$)	153	29
Fine Particulate Matter (ug/m^3)	122	44
Trace Metals (ng/m^3)		
Al	830	n.d.
As	44.5	26.2
Cl	430	197
Mn	18.9	5.5
Pb	108	48.7
Zn	160	69.2

based on Stevens *et al.* (4)

Subjects. Three cohorts of school children have been assessed including 2nd, 4th and 8th-grade students, summarized in Table 2. Eighth-grade students were tested first to take advantage of extended exposure histories and less variability in the performance of older children. Second-grade children, the youngest group which can adequately perform an extended set of computerized neurobehavioral tests, were evaluated next. The third cohort consisted of an intermediate group of 4th grade children. In each cohort, boys and girls from representative urban and rural schools were studied.

Neurobehavioral tests. The Neurobehavioral Evaluation System (NES2), a computerized test battery developed by Baker and Letz (7) was used to assess sensorimotor and cognitive function in children. Tests were translated into the Czech language and evaluated in the pilot study (8). Tests used were: finger tapping, visual digit span, continuous performance, symbol-digit substitution, pattern comparison, hand-eye coordination, switching attention and vocabulary.

Table 2   Basic statistics of the three age groups of children in three communities

Grade Age		Teplice Male/Female	Prachatice M/F	Znojmo M/F	Total
2nd	7 - 8	180/167	237/188	-	772
4th	9 - 10	91/70	70/86	96/80	493
8th	14 - 15	100/136	119/115	-	470

Parent Questionnaire. A questionnaire was administered to parents of participating children to assess (a) family demographics (e.g. parental education, occupations, type of housing, family income); (b) health history of children and parents; (c) drug, tobacco and alcohol consumption of parents; and (d) chemical exposure history of parents. These data were used in statistical analyses to control for possible confounding effects of socio-cultural, neonatal health, and other factors. Variables considered in statistical analyses are listed in Table 3.

Table 3.   Possible confounding variables

child age and gender	# occupants in flat
type of heating	private house or flat
whether child attended nursery	# smokers in flat
neonatal health problems	mother smoked before pregnancy
mother smoked during pregnancy	mother exposed to hazard in pregnancy
mother took drugs in pregnancy	parent's education level
mother's illness before pregnancy	mother's illness during pregnancy
breathing support at birth	premature birth
late hospital discharge	birth weight

Assessment of exposure. Airborne levels of trace metals were measured in the control and exposed districts in conjunction with the Czech Air Toxic Study (4). Hair and urine samples were obtained from participating second and fourth-grade children on the day of testing to measure biological levels of arsenic and mercury.

Statistical analyses. Two-way analyses of variance with factors of district and gender were used to analyze NES and parent questionnaire data. Each factor had two levels - high/low pollution districts and male/female. For biological measures of arsenic and mercury, multiple regression analyses were conducted, combining subjects from different districts. Multiple regression analyses were also used to control for potentially confounding variables derived from the parent questionnaire.

RESULTS

Eighth grade cohort. In 1992, a pilot study of 477 8th grade children from the Teplice and Prachatice was completed using questionnaires and computerized neurobehavioral tests

(NES2). Significant differences between districts in motor performance were found. Children from Prachatice performed significantly better than children from Teplice on a finger tapping test (p = 0.001). Multivariate multiple linear regression analyses were performed to determine if the observed district differences in finger-tapping could be accounted for by possible confounding effects of socioeconomic status, neonatal health or others factors. None of the potential confounders altered the significance of the district differences in finger tapping. This study is reported in detail elsewhere (9).

Second grade cohort. In 1993 772 second-grade children from the Teplice and Prachatice districts were assessed. Seven computerized neurobehavioral tests and parent questionnaires were administered. Table 4 shows the correlation of NES2 measures and potential confounding variables.

Table 4.   Correlations of NES2 measures and confounding variables (2nd graders)

Variable	Cont perfor	Digit-span	H-eye coord	Pattern compar	Switch attent	Symbol digit	Finger-tapping
1. Gender	x		x		x	x	
2. Birth weight		x					
3. # Smokers		x					
4. Smoking before pregnancy		x					
5. Parental education.		x	x		x	x	
6. Drugs/illness during pregnancy					x	x	x
7. Late hospital discharge						x	
8. Breathing support						x	

x) p ≤ 0.01 (Correlation of NES2 measure and confounder variables)

Significant correlations were found for eight items derived from the parent questionnaire. The two variables which correlated most often with neurobehavioral scores were gender and parental education. To simplify the interpretation of gender and district interactions, separate analyses of data from boys and girls were performed. The possible confounding effects of other variables were controlled in regression analyses.

Hair and urine samples were also obtained from 540 children to determine the association of neurobehavioral performance and biological measures of arsenic and mercury exposure. Levels of As and Hg observed in children from both districts were surprisingly low. The WHO level of concern for methylmercury is 10 - 20 ppm in the hair of pregnant mothers since the unborn fetus is considered to be the most susceptible to the neurotoxic effects of methylmercury (6). The average in the Teplice children was 0.885 ppm. Urinary Hg levels were similarly low.

District comparisons showed poorer performance in Prachatice children on several neuro-behavioral tests, consistent with higher hair Hg levels. Regression analyses, controlling for possible confounding factors of socioeconomic status, neonatal health and others factors, indicated significant, but weak associations of hair Hg and finger tapping, hand-eye coordination and coding performance. No meaningful associations were found with hair As or urinary measures of either metal. These findings are reported in detail elsewhere (10).

Fourth grade study. In 1994, neurobehavioral performance of 504 4th grade children (165 from Teplice, 161 from Prachatice; and 178 from Znojmo) was similarly assessed. Significant district differences in performance of digit span and symbol - digit were found - i.e. children from the mining district performed poorly compared to children from the control districts (Table 5).

Table 5.   **Selected NES2 Measures: means (SE) In Czech 4th graders: district differences**

TEST	MEASURE	Prachatice (n = 161)	Teplice (n = 165)	Znojmo (n = 178)	p-value
VISUAL DIGIT SPAN	Forward Span	5.21(.07)	4.98(.08)	5.14(.07)	.045
	Backward Span	4.31(.1)	4.05(.1)	4.39(.09)	.055
	Total (Forward+Backward)	9.52(.14)	9.02(.15)	9.53(.13)	.018
SYMBOL-DIGIT	Latency/Digit (2-best trials)	3.65(.06)	3.68(.06)	3.43(.05)	< .001
SUBSTITUTION	Latency (elapsed)	31.57(.48)	32.07(.50)	29.78(.42)	< .001

*Primary/confirmatory measures; other measures are secondary/exploratory

When scores were adjusted for potential confounder, parental education, however, these differences disappeared (Table 6).

Table 6.   **Adjusted and unadjusted pairwise district comparisons of NES2 measures in Czech 4th grade children (p-values)**

TEST	MEASURE	TEPLICE x PRACHATIC		TEPLICEx ZNOJM	
		UNADJ.	ADJ.[1]	UNADJ.	ADJ.[1]
VISUAL DIGIT SPAN	Forward Span	.025(+)	(.08)(+)	NS	NS
	Backward Span	(.051)(+)	NS	.02(+)	NS
	Total (Forward+Backward)	.011(+)	NS	.021(+)	NS
SYMBOL-DIGIT	Latency/Digit(2-best trials)	NS	NS	.001(-)	NS
SUBSTITUTION	Latency (elapsed)	NS	NS	.001(-)	NS

[1]. Model adjusted for gender, education of mother and father, type of house, # smokers, mother smoked during pregnancy, mother took drugs during pregnancy.

Table 7 illustrates the systematic association of parental education and scores of 2nd and 4th grade children on visual digit span and symbol-digit substitution tests. As the combined levels of both parents increase, the scores of children in these two tests also increase (digit span) and decrease (symbol-digit) in a linear manner.

Table 7. **Means of DIGIT SPAN (forward + backward) and latencies of SYMBOL DIGIT SUBSTITUTION for each category of education of parents, studies of 2nd and 4th grade children**

education([1]	DIGIT SPAN([2]		SYMBOL DIGIT([3]	
	2nd grade	4th grade	2nd grade	4th grade
3	7.000	8.429	47.925	33.761
4	7.240	8.595	45.851	32.541
5	7.600	9.299	44.089	31.428
6	7.733	9.462	43.122	30.269
7	8.047	10.441	40.160	28.333
8	8.000	10.368	40.700	29.597
p-value	**0.0015**	**0.00002**	**0.0023**	**0.0017**

[1] higher number of education = higher education of parents
[2] higher mean score = better result   [3] lower mean score = better result

DISCUSSION

Selected differences were found in the neurobehavioral performance of 2nd, 4th and 8th-grade Czech children living in districts with varying levels of air pollution. Possible confounding effects of socioeconomic, neonatal health, smoking in the home and other factors were assessed. District differences in finger tapping performance in 8th grade children remained after controlling for these covariates in statistical analyses. In the 2nd grade children, weak but significant associations were found in the performance of three neurobehavioral tests and hair mercury levels. These associations also remained after controlling for possible confounders. On the other hand, significant district differences in the neurobehavioral performance of 4th grade children disappeared when parental education and other covariates were controlled. Gender and parental education emerged as the two most important confounding variables in these studies of neurobehavioral performance of school children.

Extensive literature indicates that central nervous system function in children is uniquely susceptible to damage from exposure to environmental chemicals such as lead (11) and mercury (6). The effects of chemical exposure on cognitive or sensory function are often very subtle (11). Studies reviewed in this paper demonstrate the critical importance of assessing socioeconomic variables such as gender and parental education which significantly influence neurobehavioral performance. Failure to adequately control for these possible confounding variables could result in serious misinterpretation of findings in environmental health studies. Effects due to socioeconomic variables that are erroneously attributed to the chemical exposure (false positive) could be very costly to industry. On the other hand, subtle adverse effects of chemical exposures on human health, which are masked by sociocultural variables (false negatives), could be harmful to society, particularly to vulnerable subsets of the general population such as children or the elderly. Therefore it is essential to assess and control for the possible confounding effects of such variables in environmental epidemiological studies.

ACKNOWLEDGEMENTS

The Program was initiated by the Czech Ministry of the Environment in cooperation with the Ministry of Health in 1990. Many different agencies, institutes and laboratories are collaborating in this extensive research program. The program was initiated at the DG XII level of the European Communities. The U.S. Environmental Protection Agency has provided critical technical support in planning individual studies, equipment transfer, and training Czech scientists. The Teplice Program was designed as a 10-year longitudinal research project to establish an effective air monitoring program in targeted regions of the Czech Republic, to measure the effects of chemical exposure on selected health endpoints, and to recommend steps that might be taken to reduce air pollution and remediate identified health problems. We believe that only such a longitudinal study will provide the depth of knowledge necessary to adequately characterize the nature and extent of environmental health problems in Northern Bohemia. This document has been reviewed in accordance with U.S. Environmental Protection Agency policy and approved for publication. Approval does not signify that the contents necessarily reflect the views and policies of the Agency.

REFERENCES

1. Bellinger,D.Leviton,A. Waternaux,C.: Lead,IQ and social classes. *Int J Epidemiol*,1989,**18**,180-185.
2. Sram RJ. New ethical problems related to environmental pollution and behavioral changes in human populations. In: Sram RJ, Bulzenkov V, Prilipko L, Christen Y (Eds.): Ethical Issues of Molecular Genetics in Psychiatry, Springer-Verlag, Berlin, 1991, pp.94-105.
3. Gebhart JA, Dytrych Z. Tyl J., Sram RJ. On the incidence of minimal brain dysfunction syndrome in children. *Cs Psychiat* 1990, **86**: 1-6 (in Czech).
4. Stevens R, Pinto J, Metcalf J, Preuss P, Hartlage T, Novak J, Benes I, Leníček J. Czech Air Quality Monitoring and Receptor Modelling Study, Atmospheric research and exposure assessment Laboratory report, US EPA,RTP NC, August 1994
5. Fergusson JE. The Heavy Elements: Chemistry, Environmental Impact and Health Effects. Pergamon Press, New York, 1990.
6. World Health Organization. Methylmercury. Environmental Health Criteria 101.
7. Baker E,Letz R, Fidler A, *et al*. A computer-based neurobehavioral evaluation system for occupational and environmental epidemiology: Methodology and validation studies. *Neurotoxicol Teratol*, 1985,**7**: 369-377
8. Skalík I, Otto D, Hudnell HK, Sram R. Application and validation of methods for neurotoxicity testing of children in the Czech republic. Umvelthygiene-Suppl 2, GHU, Dusseldorf 1994
9. Otto D, Skalik I, Kotesovec F, Dvorakova D, Nozicka J, House D, Ratcliffe J, Sram R. Neurobehavioral performance of children living in districts of Bohemia with high and low levels of air pollution: Eight-grade pilot study. (1995, submitted).
10. Otto D, Skalik I, Subrt P, Ratcliffe J, House D, Sram R. Association of mercury exposure with neurobehavioral performance of children in Bohemia. Paper presented at 12th Int. Neurotoxicol Conf.Hot Springs, Ark,11/94 (ms. in revision)
11. Davis JM, Otto D, Weil D, Grant L. The comparative developmental neurotoxicity of lead. *Neurotoxicol Teratol,* 1990, **12**: 215-229.

EFFECTS OF SOCIOECONOMIC CONDITIONS ON RESPIRATORY SYMPTOMS AND LUNG FUNCTION TESTS IN TWO ITALIAN COMMUNITY STUDIES

Giovanni Viegi

CNR Institute of Clinical Physiology, Via Paolo Savi 8, I-56124 Pisa

SUMMARY

Two large longitudinal respiratory epidemiological surveys on general population samples in North Italy have been performed in the period 1980-1993. Socio-economic status (SES) was considered since the design of the 1st cross-sectional study with two indices: crowding and percentage of those in higher occupational positions. Low SES was associated with higher prevalence of chronic cough, phlegm and wheeze in a bivariate analysis, but not in multivariate analyses. Low SES was associated with other risk factors, such as occupational exposure to dusts, chemicals, gases and poorer home environment characteristics. Thus, analyses on respiratory symptoms and lung function tests were carried out by considering each factor as an independent confounder and not combining them into a single overall SES index.

The independent effect on respiratory outcomes of factors such as occupational exposure to dusts, chemicals, gases and poorer home environment characteristics (cooking or using a stove with fuels other than methane), active and passive smoking, low level of education, childhood and adolescence-adulthood respiratory infections, familial history of respiratory disorders were confirmed in these Italian studies. Moreover, after taking into account all these confounders or effect modifiers, the importance of residence in an urban area, characterized by higher levels of total suspended particulates and sulphur dioxide than in the rural area, was pointed out.

INTRODUCTION

The importance of socioeconomic status as risk factor for chronic respiratory disorders has been pointed out by several Authors in the last 20 years (1).

The Environmental Epidemiology Group, Pulmonary Unit, CNR Institute of Clinical Physiology, Pisa, has performed two large longitudinal epidemiological surveys in North Italy. The first survey was carried out in the Po Delta region, near Venice, before (1980-82) and after (1988-91) the start of operation of a large oil-burning central power plant. The second survey was carried out in the area of Pisa, before (1985-88) and after (1991-93) the building of a new highway connecting Pisa to Florence. Socioeconomic conditions have been considered since the design of the 1st cross-sectional study (2).

This sampling design was similarly used for the epidemiological survey in Pisa. The design was applied basically to the first cross-sectional study of the two epidemiological surveys, since the second cross-sectional study was based on those who had previously participated and on new members of their families. Finally, age and SES characteristics of subjects enrolled in the study were verified using information collected by the CNR questionnaire (3).

Aim of this paper is to review the most important information on the adverse effects of ssocioeconomicfactors on respiratory health deriving from the analyses of the Po Delta and Pisa studies.

METHODS

A stratified multistage cluster sample design was used to select families in geographic areas with different predicted levels of pollution. The purpose of the stratification was to increase the precision of the study for key variables related to risk factors and to lung function, specifically age and socioeconomic status (SES). The sampling was performed in two stages to minimize number of observations and to provide a balance between statistical precision and costs. The stratification by age and SES was carried out according to the sampling protocol of the Special Project of Chronic Obstructive Lung Disease of the Italian Research Council (4). This protocol used two SES indices for stratification: 1) "Crowding": the number of subjects living in the house divided by the number of rooms, and 2) the percentage of those in higher occupational positions based on the official classification of National Statistics Institute (ISTAT), i.e., white-collar workers, self-employed, professionals and managers (5). The age stratification was performed on the basis of the age of head of households.

Methods of respiratory health investigation were: a) in the first cross-sectional examination: a standardized interviewer-administered questionnaire developed by the Italian National Research Council (CNR), and lung function tests (forced expirograms, slow vital capacity, carbon monoxide diffusing capacity); b) in the second cross-sectional examination: determination of bronchial responsiveness to methacholine, allergological evaluation (skin prick-tests, total serum IgE level, eosinophils), some biomarkers. Methods are described in detail in the publications of the Environmental Epidemiology Group, Pulmonary Unit, CNR Institute of Clinical Physiology, Pisa, which are quoted in the text later on.

RESULTS

Main socioeconomic conditions of participants in the four cross-sectional studies are reported in Table 1. The two samples differed according to the expected urban-rural gradient: in Pisa there were more individuals with higher educational level, while there were less blue-collar workers and a lower crowding index than in Po Delta. A detailed analysis of ssocioeconomicconditions and a comparison between characteristics of expected sample and of participants in the 1st Po Delta study are reported elsewhere (2).

As regards prevalence rates of respiratory symptoms in this unpolluted area of Po Delta in Northern Italy (6), we showed that in males the prevalence rates of chronic cough and chronic phlegm increased significantly from high towards medium to low SES: 12, 16, 17% and 12, 14, 19%, respectively. In females, only prevalence rates of wheeze were significantly higher in low (6%) than in medium (2%) and in high (3%) SES.

In the following analyses we have in some way accepted the suggestion of Sherrill *et al.* (7), who, in a recent review on epidemiology of chronic obstructive pulmonary disease, affirmed that any analysis of chronic obstructive pulmonary disease (COPD) data should consider each factor as an independent confounder and not combine them into a single overall SES index.

When dealing with respiratory effects of occupational exposure in a general population sample in North Italy (8), we have confirmed that there was a significantly higher proportion of subjects in low socioeconomical conditions among those exposed than among those unexposed, both in men (46 vs 29%) and in women (24 vs 15%). Indeed, we have seen that, considering workers exposed to any dusts or chemicals or gases, non smoking women who were exposed had significantly higher prevalence rates

Table 1.   Socioeconomic characteristics (%) of two Italian population samples

	Males				Females			
	PD 1	PI 1	PD 2	PI 2	PD 1	PI 1	PD 2	PI 2
N	1573	1846	1342	1289	1711	2009	1499	1553∘
Education								
No education	11.6	13.0	5.3	4.6	24.6	20.8	11.2	13.6
Elementary	40.0	37.6	32.1	46.4	39.0	45.0	35.5	50.9
Jr High School	29.2	28.3	34.5	20.6	22.6	19.7	30.0	13.8
High School	15.0	17.4	25.0	23.5	10.7	12.0	21.1	18.5
College	2.3	3.4	3.1	4.3	1.8	2.3	2.1	3.2
Job position								
Manager	2.0	.7	1.6	3.3	.4	.2	.1	.6
White-collar	11.6	10.5	15.6	13.8	7.9	7.6	12.3	12.7
Blue-collar	30.6	22.6	24.8	20.1	15.9	13.8	16.2	8.5
Apprentice	.8	.1	.6	1.0	3.0	.5	1.2	1.1
Worker at home	.1	----	----	----	.3	.8	.2	.4
Contractor	.4	.4	.4	----	.2	.1	----	----
Professional	1.0	1.1	3.4	1.9	.1	.2	.7	.3
Self employed	19.7	10.2	18.0	9.7	9.0	5.2	10.4	5.9
Coadjutor	.8	.7	.9	.2	1.9	.8	1.2	.7
Working population	**67.0**	**46.4**	**65.3**	**49.9**	**38.7**	**29.2**	**42.3**	**30.2**
Pensioner	3.8	25.7	12.9	31.7	6.6	20.8	13.1	26.0
Housewife	.2	.5	----	.1	28.0	29.6	25.0	27.8
Student	23.7	22.6	16.7	15.3	19.4	15.8	14.6	12.2
Unemployed	3.4	3.4	4.0	1.9	4.6	3.2	2.7	2.4
Diseased	1.5	.3	.3	.9	2.4	.5	1.1	.8
Other	.4	.9	.8	.2	.3	.9	1.2	.6
Not working population	**33.0**	**53.4**	**34.7**	**50.1**	**61.3**	**70.8**	**57.7**	**69.8**
Housing Conditions								
No bathroom	5.7	5.2	6.6	1.4	1.4	7.6	5.5	2.2
No central heat.	22.7	27.6	7.8	13.7	25.0	29.9	8.4	19.4
Crowding (*	.98±.43	.80±.39	.76±.30	.72±.32	.98±.43	.76±.32	.76±.31	.70±.34

*) mean ± SD

PD 1 = Po Delta survey in 1980-82 PI 1 = Pisa survey in 1985-88
PD 2 = Po Delta survey in 1988-91 PI 2 = Pisa survey in 1991-93

of symptoms, such as dyspnea, asthma and asthma symptoms. Furthermore, 48% of non smoking women occupationally exposed had any symptom compared to 25% of those non exposed. Also reduced lung function was observed in exposed individuals. More recently (9), using the measurements of the provocative dose producing a 20% fall in forced expiratory volume in one second (PD20), significantly higher percentage of hyperreactive subjects was found among ex smoking exposed men. A borderline higher percentage of hyperreactive subjects was also found in non smoking exposed women.

On the other hand, when we assessed the effects of childhood and adolescence-adulthood respiratory infections (10), prevalence rate of low SES was 17.6% in those with childhood respiratory infections, not significantly different from those without childhood respiratory trouble (16.7%). Similarly, there was no significant difference in prevalence of low SES (15.1 vs 15.8%) among those with and those without adolescence-adulthood respiratory infections.

We obtained different results when we assessed the effects of home environment on respiratory symptoms and lung function (11). First of all, as expected, the presence of more polluting fuel for cooking and of a less modern heating device (stove) was significantly associated with a low SES. Among those with bottled gas for cooking, 29% of male and 34% of female adults belonged to the low SES group, compared with 13% and 15% of those using natural gas. Among those with stoves for heating, 28% of males and 30% of females had poor socioeconomic conditions, in contrast to 12% and 15% of those using central heating.

Using bivariate analysis, chronic cough in males and dyspnea in females were significantly associated with bottled gas for cooking. Significantly higher prevalence rates of chronic cough and phlegm in adult males and of dyspnea in females were found in those using stoves. The association of cooking and/or heating conditions with these symptoms have been confirmed using multiple logistic regression models (Table 2). Low SES was significantly included in the model only for the risk of chronic phlegm in those males using stoves for heating, while it was negatively associated with the risk of getting dyspnea in males using bottled gas for cooking. The adverse effects of home characteristics on lung function are reported in Table 3: beside small airway parameters, also the conventional FEV_1 was affected.

When the combination of home environment characteristics and passive smoking exposure were studied in those under 20 years (12), subjects with any parent smoking and with bottled gas cooking had significantly higher prevalence rates of wheeze (8 vs 1%), dyspnea (11 vs 0%), diagnosis of asthma (11 vs 3%), than those with natural gas cooking. Those with both parent smoking had significantly reduced mean values of forced end-expiratory flows (FEF_{25-75}, MEF_{50}) and peak expiratory flow. A significant interaction between kind of heating and passive smoking was present for peak flow and slope of alveolar plateau of nitrogen.

An overall evaluation of risk factors for chronic obstructive pulmonary disease in the first Po Delta survey on 2382 subjects, age 20+ years, has been recently made (13). We considered as respiratory outcome subjective tools, such as chronic cough and/or phlegm, any wheeze, effort dyspnea, attacks of shortness of breath with wheeze or diagnosis of asthma, and objective tools, such as abnormalities of one or more flow-volume curve parameters, and a complex characterized by the presence of chronic phlegm or any wheeze or dyspnea grade 2+, or diagnosed asthma or FEV_1/FVC ratio less than 60%. These outcomes entered as dependent variables in multiple logistic regression models, which confirmed the importance of such risk factors as age, ever smoking, lifetime cigarette consumption, childhood and adolescence-adulthood respiratory infections, family history for COPD, work exposure to dusts/chemicals. On the contrary, low socioeconomic condition (characterized by the position of the subject in the upper tertile of the frequency distribution of crowding and in the lower tertile of the frequency distribution of occupation) (2) was never significantly selected in the multiple logistic regression models.

Table 2.   Relationship of respiratory symptoms to home environment characteristics; odds ratios and 95% confidence intervals estimated in logistic models (10)

Symptom	Source of exposure	OR (CI)	Confounders in the model
Males			
Chronic	B	1.66 (1.12-2.46)	Age, smoking, pack-years
cough	S	1.44 (1.04-1.98)	Age, smoking, pack-years
	S+N	1.54 (1.10-2.35)	Age, smoking, pack years
	F/S+B/O	1.66 (1.04-2.65)	Age, smoking, pack years
Chronic phlegm	S	1.39 (1.01-1.91)	Age, smoking, pack-yrs, SES
Dyspnoea	B	1.81 (1.15-2.85)	Age, pack-years, SES (-), BMI
Females			
Dyspnoea	B	1.45 (1.00-2.10)	Age, pack-years, BMI
	S	1.46 (1.09-1.96)	Age, BMI
	S+N	1.58 (1.07-2.34)	Age, pack-years, BMI
	F/S+B/O	1.73 (1.12-2.67)	Age, pack-years, BMI

B = bottled gas (cooking); S = stove (heating); S+N = stove fuelled by natural gas; F/S+B/O = fan or stove fuelled by bottled gas, kerosene, wood or coal/oil; SES = socioeconomic status; BMI = body mass index; (-) = negative coefficient in the model.

Table 3.   Significantly different lung function tests in females 20+ years by type of heating, and combination of type and fuel for heating (10)

	Type of heating		Combination of type and fuel for heating			
	C	S	C+N	C+B/O	S+N	F/S+B/O
N	784	253	642	139	174	114
FEV_1	99	97	98	101 +	97	96 *
FEF_{25-75}	98	93 **	97	102 +	93	92 **
MEF_{50}	99	93 **	98 +	103 +	94	93 **
MEF_{75}	97	94	96	104	94	95
PF	100	97 *	100	98	97	98

**=p<0.01; *=p<0.05 (by ANOVA, adjusting for age, pack-years and SES); +=p<0.05 (by Duncan's multirange test) in comparison to S+N and F/S+B/O; C=central heating; S=stove; C+N=central heating fuelled by natural gas; C+B/O=central heating fuelled by bottled gas, kerosene, wood or coal/oil; FEV_1=forced expiratory volume in one second; FEF_{25-75}=forced mid-expiratory flow; MEF_{50} and MEF_{75}=maximal expiratory flow at 50% and 25% expired volume; PF=peak flow; SES=socioeconomic status; ANOVA=analysis of variance.

An occasion to test the importance of characteristics related to socioeconomic conditions, like work exposure, low education and indoor exposure, in the field of air pollution epidemiology came from a comparison of prevalence rates of respiratory symptoms in the area of Po Delta and in the area of Pisa during the first cross sectional studies, i.e., areas exposed to different levels of air pollution (14). The area of Pisa was divided in three zones: one was suburban, one was the South East part of the city (both affected by automobile exhausts from the heavily used highway connecting Pisa to Florence, that passes through a densely polluted area closely surrounded by houses), the third zone was the South West part of the city (affected also by fumes, high in sulphur dioxide (SO_2) and total suspended particulates (TSP), deriving from an industry). In fact, there was a gradient in the concentrations of air pollution: for instance, levels of TSP were around 30 $\mu g/m^3$ in Po Delta, while they ranged from 64 to 140 $\mu g/m^3$ in Pisa. When multiple logistic analyses were applied (Table 4), residence in the Pisa urban and suburban zones was significantly associated with all respiratory symptoms, except chronic phlegm, after taking into account the independent effects of host and environmental risk factors including work exposure to dusts or chemicals and fumes and a low level of education. The odds ratios for wheeze and rhinitis were the highest, especially in the urban industrial zone.

DISCUSSION

Low SES was associated with higher prevalence of chronic cough, phlegm and wheeze in a bivariate analysis, but not in multivariate analyses, in these Italian epidemiological studies. However, low SES was associated with other risk factors, such as occupational exposure to dusts, chemicals, gases and poorer home environment characteristics.

Therefore, our findings on occupational exposure (8) may also be considered as a confirmation of the negative health effects of low socioeconomical conditions. In fact, with a multivariate analysis (logistic regression), we were able to show significantly higher relative risks of getting respiratory symptoms and reduced lung function in exposed than in unexposed individuals. However, the reason for a weak association between professional exposure and bronchial reactivity in the 2nd Po Delta study (9) may be: 1) the cross sectional design and the population characteristics may not be effective enough to reveal all the adverse effects; 2) the burden of occupational exposure in a general population is not sufficient to substantially affect bronchial hyperreactivity prevalence; and 3) an increase in bronchial responsiveness after occupational exposure might be transient and not always detectable in a general population sample. Thus, there are some signals, even if weak and not homogeneous, of a relationship between occupational exposure and development of bronchial hyperreactivity.

Another potential effect of socioeconomic status derives from the observation (15) that the age of onset of asthma began after onset of employment. This can suggest that the contribution of occupational history to the development of asthma may exceed the estimates deriving from the studies of occupational asthma (16).

That occupational exposure may have long term effects has been recently demonstrated by Humerfelt and colleagues (17) in a community longitudinal survey of lung function in men aged 22-54 years followed for up to 25 years. It is therefore time to decide (18) whether occupational exposure can be considered as an established risk factor for COPD, as proposed by Becklake (19), instead than a putative risk factor, as considered by the 1984 and 1985 U.S. Surgeon General's reports on chronic obstructive lung disease.

As regards characteristics of home environment, from our findings in the Po Delta study (11-12), they may be considered as an indicator of socioeconomical condition, therefore they, along with passive smoking, should be taken into account in multivariate analyses for factors affecting natural history of chronic obstructive lung disease. Effects of home environment on respiratory symptoms were also investigated in a general population sample living in Pisa, Middle Italy (20). People were divided into four groups, according to combination of different fuels for cooking, heating and type of heating. These results confirmed and in some way extended our previous observations in an unpolluted rural area of North Italy, because, as mentioned before, more numerous factors were taken into account in logistic models and the independent effects of home environment characteristics were still found.

When we considered childhood and adolescence-adulthood respiratory infections (10), i.e. a putative risk factor for COPD (19), we observed that these risk factors for COPD were not associated with low SES. Thus, it appears that childhood-adulthood respiratory infections are independently associated with the outcome represented by chronic respiratory symptoms or impaired lung function.

In the overall evaluation of risk factors for chronic obstructive pulmonary disease in the Po Delta study (13), low socioeconomic condition (characterized by the position of the subject in the upper tertile of the frequency distribution of crowding and in the lower tertile of the frequency distribution of occupation) (2) was never significantly selected in the multiple logistic regression models, therefore it did not appear to be an independent contributor for COPD in our population. We checked whether low SES was significantly associated with the other risk factors investigated, but we found only a significant difference for occupational exposure to dust/chemicals between low and medium-high SES, both in men (37.5% vs 27.4%, p=0.006) and in women (15.3% vs 9.4%, p=0.008). Indeed, the lack of association of low SES with respiratory symptoms/diseases and lung impairment may be due to two reasons: 1) the crowding and occupational components may not be adequate for investigating a possible relationship of SES with respiratory outcomes; 2) there may not be enough SES variability in the study population for an effect to be noticed. On the other hand, this variable was proven to be effective in describing the socioeconomical condition of the sample with respect to the census data of the general population living in the area (2). Further, when socioeconomic characteristics of participants from questionnaire information were examined in the three SES strata used in the sampling procedure, significant differences for specific job position, education and housing conditions between low and high SES were found: even crowding was significantly different, but the index was not widely distributed (2).

Thus, our current results point out the importance of collecting more precisely information on various components of SES, as proposed by Sherrill et al (7), in order to consider each factor as an independent confounder and not to combine them into a single overall SES index.

However, as pointed out by the results of Lange et al (21), who were able to show a significant effect of low education on the risk of developing chronic mucus hypersecretion in female smokers, there may be the possibility that education is a better indicator of SES than crowding and percentage of those in higher occupational positions. This aspect is discussed in more detail in the review of Carrozzi (1). Indeed, when we considered the two first surveys in Po Delta and in Pisa, low education showed an increased odds ratio for getting respiratory symptoms than high education (Table 4). Further, the multiple logistic analyses reported in Table 4 are important because they indicate that neither host nor environmental risk factors obscured the independent negative effect of urban residence on almost all respiratory symptoms.

Table 4. Effects of risk factors for respiratory symptoms, odds ratio and confidence intervals[a] (19)

Risk factor[b]	Cough	Phlegm	Wheeze	SOBWHZ[c]	Dyspnea	Rhinitis
Sex	--	1.4 (1.2-1.8)	--	--	0.4 (0.3-0.5)	--
Age	1.3 (1.1-1.6)	1.3 (1.0-1.6)	1.2 (1.0-1.4)	--	4.2 (3.6-4.9)	1.3 (1.1-1.6)
Ever smoking	3.5 (2.8-4.3)	3.8 (3.0-4.9)	2.0 (1.6-2.4)	--	1.5 (1.2-1.7)	--
Pack-years	2.7 (2.1-3.3)	2.5 (2.0-3.2)	2.5 (2.0-3.2)	1.5 (1.1-2.1)	1.9 (1.5-2.4)	--
Respiratory, familial	1.3 (1.1-1.6)	--	1.3 (1.1-1.6)	--	1.3 (1.2-1.5)	1.2 (1.0-1.4)
Allergic, familial	--	--	1.4 (1.1-1.6)	1.8 (1.4-2.2)	0.8 (0.7-0.9)	1.7 (1.5-2.1)
Work exposure	1.3 (1.1-1.6)	1.4 (1.1-1.6)	1.5 (1.3-1.8)	1.5 (1.2-1.9)	1.9 (1.6-2.3)	1.4 (1.2-1.7)
Low education	1.3 (1.0-1.6)	1.3 (1.0-1.6)	1.3 (1.0-1.6)	1.3 (1.0-1.6)	1.5 (1.2-1.9)	0.7 (0.6-0.8)
Indoor exposure	1.2 (1.0-1.4)	--	--	1.2 (1.0-1.5)	1.2 (1.1-1.4)	--
Zone						
Cascina	1.2 (1.1-1.3)	--	1.4 (1.3-1.5)	1.2 (1.1-1.3)	1.3 (1.2-1.4)	1.6 (1.5-1.7)
Pisa-SE	1.4 (1.3-1.5)	--	2.0 (1.8-2.1)	1.4 (1.3-1.5)	1.6 (1.5-1.8)	2.5 (2.3-2.7)
Pisa-SW	1.7 (1.6-1.8)	--	2.8 (2.6-3.0)	1.6 (1.5-1.8)	2.1 (1.9-2.2)	4.0 (3.7-4.3)

[a]=Derived from multiple logistic models, compared to subjects without the risk factors.
[b]=Age, >40 years; pack-years, >20; respiratory/allergic, familial: familial history for respiratory/allergic disorders; work exposure: to specific dusts/chemicals/fumes; low education: less than high school degree; indoor exposure: to stove and/or fuel other than natural gas.
[c]=SOBWHZ=attacks of wheezing dyspnea.

84

In conclusion, our recent reports (13-14) are further confirmation of the multifactorial character of COPD (7): this notion is particularly important in air pollution epidemiology because the data were collected in a rural unpolluted area and in a medium-size urban area, mostly involved by automobile exhausts. If we consider that morbidity and mortality of COPD are still increasing, in spite of improvement in medical treatment (22), our results indicate the necessity of a comprehensive strategy of preventive medicine, not limited to smoking cessation campaigns.

ACKNOWLEDGEMENT

This work was supported in part by the National Research Council, Targeted Project "Prevention and Control of Disease Factors - SP2 - Contract No 91.00171.PF41"; the CNR-ENEL Project "Interactions of the Energy System with Human Health and Environment", Rome, Italy; the Contract No. BMH1-CT92-0849 (BIOMED1) between the European Economic Community and the University of Pisa, Italy; Boehringer Ingelheim Italia.

REFERENCES

1. Carrozzi L. Evaluation of socioeconomic factors in respiratory epidemiology. In Jantunen MJ, Viegi G, Nolan C (Eds) *Socioeconomic and Cultural Factors in Air Pollution Epidemiology*. **EC Air Pollution Epidemiology Report Series No: 8,** 1997, 27-34.
2. Carrozzi L, Giuliano G, Viegi G, *et al.* The Po River delta epidemiological study of osbtructive lung disease: sampling methods, environmental and population characteristics. *Eur J Epidem* 1990;**6**:191-200.
3. Fazzi P, Viegi G, Paoletti P, *et al.* Comparison between two standardized questionnaires and pulmonary function tests in a group of workers. *Eur J Respir Dis* 1982;**63**:168-169.
4. Circella AM. L'indagine epidemiologica come sistema di controllo della salute: un modello di lavoro per il Sottoprogetto BPCO. Atti del Convegno Nazionale del Progetto Finalizzato di Medicina Preventiva del CNR. Roma, 17-20 Maggio 1978.
5. Istituto Centrale di Statistica. Classificazione delle Attività Economiche. Metodi e norme: serie C, n. 5, Roma 1971.
6. Viegi G, Paoletti P, Prediletto R, Carrozzi L, *et al.* Prevalence of respiratory symptoms in an unpolluted area of Northern Italy. *Eur Respir J* 1988;**1**:311-318.
7. Sherrill D, Lebowitz MD, Burrows B. Epidemiology of chronic obstructive pulmonary disease. *Clin Chest Med* 1990;**11**:375-387.
8. Viegi G, Prediletto R, Paoletti P, Carrozzi L, *et al.* Respiratory effects of occupational exposure in a general population sample in North Italy. *Am Rev Respir Dis* 1991;**143**:510-515.
9. Viegi G, Fialdini AM, Vellutini M, Carrozzi L, *et al.* Bronchial reactivity in a general population of North Italy: relationships with occupational exposure. *Monaldi Arch Chest Dis* 1994;**49**:15-18.
10. Paoletti P, Prediletto R, Carrozzi L, Viegi G, *et al.* Effects of childhood and adolescence-adulthood respiratory infections in a general population. *Eur Respir J* 1989;**2**:428-436.
11. Viegi G, Paoletti P, Carrozzi L, *et al.* Effects of home environment on respiratory symptoms and lung function in a general population sample in North Italy. *Eur Respir J* 1991;**4**:580-586.
12. Viegi G, Carrozzi L, Paoletti P, *et al.* Effects of some indoor environmental factors on respiratory symptoms and lung function in a sample of young non smokers in North Italy. *Aerobiologia* 1991;**7**:152-159.
13. Viegi G, Carrozzi L, Di Pede F, *et al.* Risk factors for chronic obstructive pulmonary disease in a North Italian rural area. *Eur J Epidemiol* 1994;**10**:1-7.
14. Viegi G, Paoletti P, Carrozzi L, *et al.* Prevalence rates of respiratory symptoms in Italian general population samples exposed to different levels of air pollution. *Environ Health Perspect* 1991;**94**:95-99.
15. Viegi G, Baldacci S, Vellutini M, Carrozzi L, *et al.* Prevalence rates of diagnosis of asthma in general population samples of Northern and Central Italy. *Monaldi Arch Chest Dis* 1994;**49**:191-196.
16. Chan-Yeung M, Lam S. State of Art. Occupational asthma. *Am Rev Respir Dis* 1986;**133**:686-703.
17. Humerfelt S, Gulsvik S, Skjaerven R, *et al.* Decline in FEV1 and airflow limitation related to occupational exposure in men of an urban community. *Eur Respir J* 1993;**6**:1095-1103.
18. Viegi G, Paoletti P. How to assess long-term effects of occupational exposure. *Eur Respir J* 1993;**6**:1088-1089.
19. Becklake MR. Occupational exposures: evidence for a causal association with chronic obstructive pulmonary disease. *Am Rev Respir Dis* 1989;**140**:S85-S91.
20. Viegi G, Carrozzi L, Paoletti P, *et al.* Effects of home environment on respiratory symptoms of a general population sample in Middle Italy. *Arch Environ Health* 1992;**47**:64-70.
21. Lange P, Groth S, Nyboe A, *et al.* Determinants of chronic mucus hypersecretion in a general population with special reference to the type of tobacco smoked. *Int J Epidemiol* 1989;**18**:882-887.
22. Higgins MW, Speizer FE, *et al.* The rise in chronic obstructive pulmonary disease mortality. *Am Rev Respir Dis* 1989;**140** (Suppl):S1-S107.

SOCIOECONOMIC AND OCCUPATIONAL DIFFERENCES IN RESPIRATORY MORTALITY AND DISABILITY IN FINLAND

Veijo Notkola, Kaj Husman
University of Helsinki, Department of Sociology
Kuopio Regional Institute of Occupational Health, PL 93, 70701 Kuopio, Finland

INTRODUCTION AND AIMS OF THE STUDY

Socioeconomic mortality differences or mortality differences associated with occupational status are very clear in almost all countries in Europe. There are some differences in magnitude of mortality differences. The smallest inequalities in mortality in Europe are observed in Norway and in Denmark (1, 2). Socioeconomic differences can be found not just in mortality but also in morbidity.

According to the cause of death, the socioeconomic differences in mortality are very similar, with few exceptions. However, it can be assumed that due to the higher smoking prevalence, poor housing and living conditions, life-style, and heavier working conditions, the ssocioeconomicdifferences in respiratory mortality and morbidity are greater than in all causes of mortality and morbidity. In several studies in Europe it has been shown that in particular blue collar workers compared to the white collar workers have significantly higher respiratory mortality and morbidity (3,4,5,6).

In Finland socioeconomic differences in mortality are also clear (7). Mortality has declined among the over-50-year-old population in Finland during the 1980s, but at the same time the socioeconomic differences in mortality seem either to have increased or remained stable during the past few decades (7,8). In Finland the mortality of manual labourers is highest, followed by farmers, then lower white-collar employees; mortality is lowest among upper white-collar employees.

There are also clear socioeconomic differences in morbidity in Finland. The prevalence of chronic illness limiting work ability was highest among farmers, and the second highest among manual labourers. The health status of upper white-collar employees was clearly the best (9, 10, 11). Among men the age-adjusted prevalence of respiratory morbidity was highest among manual labourers (11). Among women the prevalence of respiratory morbidity was highest among farmers (11). The difference between the labourers and other groups was greater due to respiratory diseases than to other diseases. In Finland the incidence of disability pensions varies by occupational class, too (12).

The aim of this study was to analyse in particular the differences in socioeconomic and occupational mortality and disability as regards respiratory mortality during the 1980s in Finland.

METHODS

The study was based on the Finnish population census records of 1970, 1975, 1980, and 1985, linked with all death certificates during 1971-1991 (7,13). The disability pensions from the National Insurance Institution were available for the period 1986-1990. The disability pension can be awarded to persons aged 16-64 who cannot perform their customary work or some other comparable work which with regard to age, occupational skills and other factors can be regarded as suitable and guaranteeing a reasonable income (14). In the disability pensions, the analysis was limited to the population aged under 55 years, because after that age there are also other early retirement pensions which affect the incidence of disability pension in Finland. The linkage of data sets was carried out by Statistics Finland.

The causes of death were classified according to the 9th revision of the International Classification of diseases. Diseases of the respiratory system included ICD codes 460-519 among persons aged 35-64 years, and among persons 60 and above, the classification was the following: all respiratory diseases (= ICD 460-519), pneumonia (480-485) and other respiratory diseases. In the case of respiratory diseases also more precise cause of death classification was used.

Socioeconomic classification was based on occupational class. The following large occupational categories were used as the indication of socioeconomic class: Upper white-collar employees, lower white-collar employees, labourers, and farmers (7). Mortality and morbidity differences were analysed by using the exact code of occupation in the three-digit level of occupational class (13).

In the case of large occupational classes, the theory of generalized linear models was applied in the calculation of mortality differences by using the GLIM system (15). Indirect standardization (standardized mortality ratio or standardized disability ratio) was used in the calculation of occupational mortality and disability ratios (16).

RESULTS

Socioeconomic Mortality Differences

There were clear socioeconomic differences among the working-aged population in respiratory mortality in Finland (Table 1). Particularly among male workers the respiratory mortality was 3-4 times higher than the mortality of upper white-collar employees. The same difference could also be found among women, although the difference was smaller.

Table 1.   Relative age-standardized total mortality and respiratory mortality by socioeconomic class in 1981-1990 in Finland (upper white-collar employees = 100, men and women aged 35-64)

	Total mortality	Respiratory diseases
Men		
Upper white-collar workers	100	100
Lower white-collar workers	141	189
Labourers	201	358
Farmers	157	271
Women		
Upper white-collar workers	100	100
Lower white-collar workers	111	123
Labourers	140	206
Farmers	129	219

Source: Valkonen, T., Martelin, T., Rimpelä, A., Notkola, V., Savela, S. Socioeconomic mortality differences in Finland 1981-90. Statistics Finland. Population 1993:1.

The socioeconomic mortality differences due to respiratory diseases were bigger than the socioeconomic differences in total mortality.

There were also clear socioeconomic differences in respiratory mortality among the population aged 60 years and above in Finland (Table 2). However, the differences were not as pronounced as in the working-aged population. Compared to the all cause mortality the socioeconomic differences due to respiratory mortality were greater. There were clear socioeconomic differences in mortality both among men and women, but among men the differences were greater. The mortality differences due to pneumonia and to other respiratory diseases were clear. In the case of other respiratory diseases, greater variation was found in this regard among men than among women.

Table 2. **Relative age-standardized total mortality and respiratory mortality by socioeconomic class in 1981-1990 in Finland (upper white-collar employees = 100, men and women aged 60 years and above)**

	Total mortality	Respiratory diseases	Pneumonia	Other respiratory diseases
Men				
Upper white-collar workers	100	100	100	100
Lower white-collar workers	121	139	123	161
Labourers	144	212	158	291
Farmers	124	189	151	243
Women				
Upper white-collar workers	100	100	100	100
Lower white-collar workers	112	112	109	119
Labourers	128	135	135	136
Farmers	123	146	152	130

Source: Valkonen, T., Martelin, T., Rimpelä, A., Notkola, V., Savela, S. Socioeconomic mortality differences in Finland 1981-90. Statistics Finland. Population 1993:1.

Occupational Mortality Differences

The respiratory mortality was particularly high in seven different male occupations (Table 3). Cleaning work, farm work, dock work and assistant house building work seem to explain the increased mortality due to respiratory diseases. On the other hand, during the study period there were no female occupations among women aged 25-64 years in which the mortality was above average of females due to respiratory diseases in period 1981-1991. However, if the follow-up time was extended for the period 1971-1991 there was five occupations also among women whose mortality was above average (Table 3).

In the case of respiratory mortality it is possible to use more precise classification of death. It seems to be that by using more precise classification of deaths the mortality differences are still bigger between occupations. The relative age-adjusted mortality due to chronic obstructive pulmonary disease among males aged 25-64 years during 1971-1991 was high in following occupations: cleaners & cleaning managers (SMR 446, CI = 198-884), asphalt roofing workers (SMR 322, CI = 129-670), engine-room crew (SMR = 244, CI = 111-467), labourers not classified elsewhere (SMR = 191, CI = 162-225), garden and park workers (SMR 185, CI = 113-287), farm workers (SMR 180, CI = 143-225), assisting house building workers (SMR 173, CI = 149-201), other assisting house building workers (SMR 173, CI = 149-201), other guards (SMR 156, CI = 121-200), forestry workers (SMR 145, CI = 127-165) and farmers (SMR 110, CI = 106-116). Among females aged 25-64 years the obstructive pulmonary mortality was increased among other occupations in textiles (SMR 504 CI = 183-1107), knitting machine operators (SMR 278 CI = 101-612), assisting house building workers (SMR 255, CI = 139-430), other machine and metalware occupations (SMR 241, CI = 110-461), waiters and headwaiters (SMR 231, CI = 139-362), plywood and fibreboard workers (SMR 207, CI = 111-357) and office clerks (SMR 135, CI = 104-175). Most of these occupations were blue collar occupations even among females.

Table 3.   The relative age-adjusted increased mortality among the male working population aged 25-64 years due to respiratory diseases by occupation in Finland in 1981-1991 (The mortality of economically active male population in 1975 and 1980 = 100) and among females 1971-1991 (The mortality of the economically active females 1970 = 100).

	Standardized Mortality Ratio (1981-1991)	95% Confidence Interval
Men		
Cleaners & cleaning managers	272	99-597
Farm workers	181	107-287
Dockers	176	109-269
Labourers not elsewhere classified	163	113-228
Assistant house building workers	140	109-177
Guards	125	74-199
Other assistant house building workers	118	80-168
All employees	68	64-72
Women	(1971-1991)	
Waiters, headwaiters	216	158-288
Assisting building workers	174	114-256
Plywood and fibreboard workers	159	105-232
Housekeepers	151	123-182
Farmers	115	102-129
All employees	100	

Source: Notkola, V., Pajunen, A., Leino-Arjas, P.: Occupational mortality and disability differences in Finland 1971-1991.

Among men more define cause specific mortality classification could be used. In particular and also extremely high was mortality in some occupations due to pneumoconioses and other diseases due to external agents among the male working population aged 25-64 years in 1971-1991. The standardized mortality ratio for insulation workers was 7150 (CI = 3258-13648), mining and quarrying work it was 4047 (CI = 2152-6947), moulders (SMR 1698, CI = 535-4003), smelting and foundry work (SMR 951,

CI = 433-1815), other machine and metalware occupations (SMR 776, CI = 248-1831), other manufacturing work (SMR 698, CI = 223-1646), turners, toolmakers and machine tool-setters (SMR 319, CI = 102-752) and in other construction work standardized mortality ratio was 233 (CI = 128-394). It is obvious that in some of these occupations there has been clear exposure to the asbestos.

Occupational Disability Differences Due to Respiratory Diseases

During the study period (1986-1990) the number of disability pensions due to respiratory diseases among men was 1093 and among women 960. There were several different occupations of both men and women in which the incidence of disability pension due to respiratory diseases was clearly higher than the average. For men, the excess relative risk of disability pension was five-fold among chimney sweeps and bakers (Table 4). The mortality in bakery work was a high also for women. For men, work in the metal industry was related to an excess risk of disability pension. For women, farming seemed to be a very important cause of the excess risk of disability pension due to respiratory diseases. There were altogether 960 disability cases among women during the study period; 200 of these disability pensions were granted to female agricultural workers (Table 4). Other women's high risk occupations were ones in which the exposure at work probably causes the excess risk of disability.

DISCUSSION

There are very big differences in mortality and morbidity by occupational status in Europe. Among the biggest of these mortality differences is in respiratory mortality. In most cases the order of occupational classes in mortality and in morbidity is the same in all countries, with blue collar workers having the highest mortality, followed by farmers, lower white collar employees and upper white-collar employees in that order. This order could also be found from this study. In addition according to this study, there are certain occupations in Fin-land where the respiratory mortality is particularly high. The reasons for this difference could be life-style factors such as smoking, alcohol consumption, dietary habits, and living conditions, but also exposure at work. The working conditions of labourers and agricultural workers are in general dustier and include more respiratory irritants than the working conditions of upper white-collar workers. Even though the number of cases of occupational mortality among working aged men was small (Table 3) all the occupations with relatively high SMRs to respiratory diseases were such that they confirm the conclusions drawn above.

All the seven male occupations with relatively high SMRs represent the lowest socioeconomic groups (blue collar workers and agricultural workers) and one can assume that their work environment contains respiratory irritants, and that possibly their life-style is not very healthy.

The differences in occupational disability due to respiratory diseases among men and women were quite clear in Finland in the 1980s. Disability pensions are not only related to health, but also to e.g. social conditions, physical load at work and to employment situation. Manninen and Notkola (17) have shown in a prospective study that perceived health status and morbidity predicted quite well disability pensions.

There are no earlier reports on the risk of disability due to respiratory diseases by occupation. In this study male and female bakers had a fivefold disability risk. The risk of both men and women engaged in farming was two to five times higher than the incidence in the whole economically active population in

Finland in the 1980s. Even though we can not determine the risk for disability pension attributable to the work environment, we know that both bakers and agricultural workers are at high risk for work-related exposures (18, 19). This might be one reason explaining the elevated SDRs in these occupations in 1986-1990 in Finland. Similarly, there are respiratory irritants in the work environment of most of the other occupations with SDR over 200 (3, 20).

Table 4. **The relative age-adjusted increased incidence of disability pensions by occupation 1985 under 55-year-old aged population due to respiratory diseases in Finland in 1986-1990 (The incidence of disability pensions in the labour force 1985 = 100)**

	Standardized Disability Ratio	95% confidence interval
Men		
Chimney sweeps (*	569	182-1341
Bakers	509	232-971
Plastics product makers	417	199-771
Metal smelting furnace men	412	165-855
Blacksmiths	380	136-835
Forestry workers	302	226-395
Labourers not classified elsewhere	278	159-453
Sheet-metal workers	268	185-375
Farm workers	265	132-476
Furniture makers	254	109-503
Assistant house building workers	253	175-357
Welders and flame cutters	227	153-324
Truck drivers	226	134-357
Plumbers	184	117-277
Turners, toolmakers and machine tool setters	166	106-249
All	**95**	**88-101**
Women		
Bakers	632	440-880
Spinning machine operators	494	183-1085
Farm workers	482	294-746
Plywood makers	293	117-609
Typographers, etc.	287	104-630
Hairdressers and barbers (*	271	160-429
Warehouse workers	268	150-443
Farmers (*	260	187-354
Farm workers (*	211	176-249
Waiters, headwaiters	210	117-347
Cleaners	117	94-144
All	**82**	**76-89**

*) Includes entrepreneurs
Source: Notkola, V., Pajunen, A., Leino-Arjas, P.: Occupational mortality and disability differences in Finland 1971-1991.

Based on the results of this study we can conclude that occupational factors have to take account always when respiratory mortality and morbidity are going to be studied.

REFERENCES

1. Kunst A, Mackenbach J. International Variation in the Size of Mortality Differences Associated with occupational Status. *Intern J Epid* 1994;**23**, 737-741.
2. Leclerc A. Differential mortality by cause of death: comparison between selected European countries. In: Fox J (ed.). Health Inequalities in European Countries. Aldershot. Gower, 1989.
3. Heederick D, Kromhout H, Burema J, Biersteker K, Kromhout D. Occupational exposure and 25-year incidence rate of non-specific lung disease: the Zuptan Study. *Intern J Epid* 1990;**19**, 945-952.
4. Vestbo J, Knudsen K, Rasmussen F. The effect of smoking and occupation on chamges in respiratory symptoms in middle-aged Danish men. *Eur Respirat J* 1990;**13**, 880-885.
5. Moser K, Goldblatt P. Occupational mortality of women aged 15-59 years at death in England and Wales. *J Epid Community Health* 1991;**45**, 117-124
6. Leon D, Smith G, Shipley M, Strachan D. Adult height and mortality in London: early life, socioeconomic confounding, or shrinkage? *J Epid Community Health* 1995;**49**, 5-9
7. Valkonen T, Martelin T, Rimpelä A, Notkola V, Savela S. Socioeconomic mortality differences in Finland 1981-90. Statistics Finland. Population 1993:**1**.
8. Notkola V, Martikainen P, Leino P. Time trends in mortality in forestry and construction workers in Finalnd 1970-85 and impact of adjustment for socioeconomic variables. *J Epid Community Health* 1993;**47**, 186-191.
9. Notkola V, Husman K, Susitaival P, Taattola K. Morbidity and risk factors of Finnish farmers. *Scand J Work and Environ Health* 1992;**18**, Suppl 2, 51-54.
10. Lahelma E, Manderbacka K, Rahkonen O, Sihvonen A-P. Ill health and its social patterning in Finland, Norway and Sweden. Research reports 27. Jyväskylä 1993. National Research and Development Centre for Welfare and Health. Helsinki. Finland.
11. Perkiö M, Notkola V. Morbidity, health behaviour and use of health services among farmers in Finland 1992. In: Susitaival P (ed.): Farming and occupational health in Finland in 1992. Helsinki: Publications of the Social Insurance Institution, Finland, ML:133,1994. (In Finnish).
12. Hytti H. The causes and background factors in the development of disability pensions in Finland. Helsinki: Publications of the Social Insurance Institution, Finland, M:87,1993. (In Finnish).
13. Notkola V, Pajunen A, Leino-Arjas P. Occupational mortality and disability differences in Finland 1971-1991. *Statistics Finland. Health* 1995:**4**. Helsinki 1995.
14. Statistical Yearbook of the Social Insurance Institution 1993. The Social Insurance Institution 1994 (In Finnish).
15. Payne CD (ed.) The GLIM System, Release 3.77. Manual. Oxford: The Numerical Algorithms Group, Royal Statistical Society, 1985.
16. Armitage D. Statistical Methods in Medical Research. Blackwell Scientific Publications, Oxford 1980.
17. Manninen P, Notkola V. The incidence of disability pensions among farmers in Finland 1980-1990. In: Susitaival P (ed.): Farming and occupational health in Finland in 1992. Helsinki: Publications of the Social Insurance Institution, Finland, ML:133,1994. (In Finnish).
18. Thiel H. Problems of occupationally induced respiratory allergies as exemplified by bakers' asthma. *Dermatosen in Beruf und Umwelt* 1987; **35**, 81-91.
19. Terho E, Husman K, Vohlonen I (eds.).: Work-related respiratory diseases among Finnish farmers. *Eur J Respirat Dis* 1987;**71,** suppl No 152.
20. Lyngenbo O, Groth S, Olsen O, Rossing N. Occupational lung function impairment in never-smoking Danish welders. *Scand J Soc Med* 1989;**12**, 157-164.

IMPROVING THE COMPARABILITY OF SOCIOECONOMIC MEASURES ACROSS EUROPE

Anton E. Kunst and *Johan P. Mackenbach*

Department of Public Health, Erasmus University, P.O. Box 1738, NL-3000 DR Rotterdam

INTRODUCTION

The purpose of this paper is give recommendations for the measurement of socioeconomic factors in international projects on the health effects of air pollution.

To do some justice to the great diversity of studies in air pollution epidemiology, we assume 3 different types of studies (and ignore time series analyses):

1. studies in which socioeconomic factors can be measured at the individual level and with considerable detail (just like measurements of smoking histories and time activities patterns);

2. studies in which socioeconomic factors can be measured at the individual level, but where a detailed measurement of these factors is not feasible or not considered necessary;

3. purely 'ecologic' studies, in which socioeconomic factors are measured at the area level, either for the selection of study areas or as control variables in later statistical analyses.

Recommendations for the first two types of studies are given in section 2, and for the third type of study in section 3.

We concentrate on the measurement of 'socioeconomic status' and its three core indicators: education, income and occupation. Since each of these core indicators is an independent predictor of health (1) each indicator is a potential confounder or effect modifier in air pollution epidemiology. For each indicator separately, therefore, the need and feasibility of its inclusion in studies on the health effects of air pollution should be considered. We will therefore discuss the measurement of each socioeconomic indicator.

Our recommendations are based on our experiences with international comparisons on socioeconomic inequalities in health (2-4). More details on the recommendations that are given in this paper can be found in a discussion document that we have written at the request of the WHO Regional Office for Europe (5).

THE MEASUREMENT OF SOCIOECONOMIC STATUS AT THE INDIVIDUAL LEVEL

Education

Information on the educational achievement emphasizes differences between people in knowledge, skills and attitudes.

Detailed measurement: A common way of measuring educational level is to ask each individual for the highest type of education that has successfully been completed (with diploma, if applicable). If possible, this measure takes into account not only general education but also technical and vocational education, and not only full-time education but also part-time study or training after leaving school.

International comparability of educational levels can be improved in two ways:

1. Combining educational categories according to the knowledge level that they embody. An internationally applicable classification is: (a) no education completed; (b) elementary education; (c) lower secondary education; (d) upper secondary education; (e) post-secondary education (6).

2. Expressing the knowledge level of an educational category by means of the internationally applicable concept of *grade*, by which is meant the minimum number of years of education that is formally required to complete that educational category.

Most of the measurement effort relates to the need to determine for all persons their precise educational level. Additional work is required for making the measurements internationally comparable.

Simple measurement: A lot of data processing work could be saved by asking for the educational level with a question with pre-fixed answer categories instead of with an open question. Often, the avoidance of coding work justifies the resulting loss of accuracy.

Simpler measures are obtained by asking for the number of years of education that a person has attended school full-time, or the age at leaving school. A disadvantage of these measures is that they do not take into account the number of times that a person had to repeat a grade, nor the type, and therefore the level, of school that was attended.

Table 1. **Educational differences in the prevalence of 'less than good' general health and in the prevalence of 'any long-standing health problem'. A comparison of two educational measures. Great Britain, 1988, men 15-64 years. Source: Kunst *et al.* (7)**

Educational measure	% with health 'less than good'	% with any long-standing problem
Level completed		
- College and more	26.8	29.0
- lower ([a]	32.6 (1.21)	32.7 (1.13)
Age left school		
- 19 years or more	24.0	28.4
- younger ([a]	32.2 (1.34)	32.2 (1.13)

[a]) Between brackets ratio low/high educational level

Example: An example of two ways to measure educational level is given in Table 1. Male respondents 15 to 64 years in a British survey were classified according to (1) the highest level they completed and (2) the age they left school. In the table, a comparison is made between the about 30 % of men with the highest educational level (college education or more, left school at 19 years or later) all men with lower education. For both ways of classifying men, those with higher educational level were found to suffer less often from poor health. In this example, the simpler educational measure (age left school) appeared to show health differences that are at least as large as those observed with the more sophisticated measure.

Income

It is common to use information on income as complementary to information on education because of its emphasis on access to scarce material goods and services.

Detailed measurement: As a measure of access to goods and services, income level can best be calculated by:

- adding all income components (this yields total income);
- subtracting tax deductions and social security contributions (disposable income);
- adding the incomes of all household members (household disposable income);
- adjusting for the size of the household (equivalent disposable income). A simple and internationally applicable formula for the correction for household size consists of dividing the household income by the square root of the number of household members.

Care should be taken that the incomes of all household members are counted and that the respondents take into account the most relevant income components such as wages and salaries, interests, pensions and transfer payments.

International comparability of income levels can be attained in two ways:

1. converting the income levels into a common currency, such as ECU's, by means of purchasing power parities;
2. constructing for each country individually a hierarchy of income groups of the same population share, e.g., income deciles or quintiles.

Most of the measurement effort relates to the extensive set of questions that is needed for a detailed assessment of income levels. It may be questioned whether this is worth the effort: survey questions on income typically meet high non-response rates and, moreover, willing respondents may not report income accurately or validly.

Simple measurement: Health interview surveys from many countries measure the income level of the respondents by just one or two questions on the household disposable income. Such a simple question obviously yields less accurate information. It is not worthless, however, because large health differences are usually found even according to this simple income measure (8).

An alternative to the measurement of income is to use proxy measures for material living standards. A wide variety of such indicators have been used in health inequality research. Perhaps most appropriate for use in air pollution epidemiology are proxy measures of long-term living standards, such as the possession of durable consumption goods, car ownership, house ownership, or indicators of the quality of housing. These indicators have the advantage that they are more stable over time whereas income levels may vary substantially. In addition, questions on house ownership etc do not create the problems of non-response and inaccuracy that are typical for questions on income.

On the other hand, the validity of these measures as indicators of living standards is doubtful. The association between these indicators and health (9-11) reflects probably not only the effect of low living standards, but also the effect of other health-related factors. For example, the often reported lower mortality among homeowners probably reflects not only the higher living standards of homeowners but also the differences between them and tenants in geographical mobility and selection for health in obtaining mortgages.

International comparability of proxy measures of living standards may be poor. Indicators that are considered to be reasonably valid in one country may be invalid in other countries.

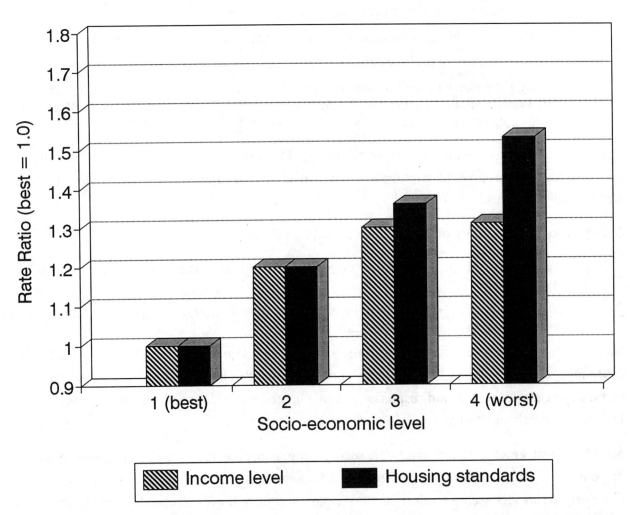

Figure 1.   **Age-standardised mortality rates by income level and by housing quality. Finland, 1981-1985, men 60 years and older. Source: Martelin (12)**

Example: An example of using income and a proxy measure is presented in Figure 1. In a Finnish study, men older than 60 years were classified from 'best' to 'worst' according to their income level, and according to the quality of the house, where they lived. High mortality rates were associated with both low income and substandard housing. The largest mortality differences were observed when men were classified according to housing quality. A possible explanation is that housing quality reflects wealth accumulated over the men's life, and the accumulated wealth is more relevant to the elderly's health than their current income.

Occupation

Occupation is perhaps the most comprehensive socioeconomic indicator. It is certainly the most complicated one to measure. We should stress that occupation is treated here as an indicator of socioeconomic status, and not as an indicator of work-related exposure to toxic compounds.

Detailed measurement: Essential to a detailed measurement of occupation is the classification of persons according to occupational title ('accountant', 'bricklayer' etc) such as in the International Standard Classification of Occupations. If feasible, additional information is obtained on employment status (self-employed or in employment) and supervisory status (number of subordinates).

It is common to classify economically inactive men (unemployed, retired, disabled etc) according to their last or longest held occupation. Women can be classified according to their own occupation, but married and co-habiting women can also be classified according to the occupation of their partner. Both ways of classifying women are valid and there is no clear preference for either one. Perhaps most important for the present purposes is that the largest health differences are most often found when married and co-habiting women are classified with reference to their partner's occupation (13,14).

International comparability of occupational data can be improved in two ways:

1. Combining occupations according to an internationally applicable scheme of 'social classes' (professionals, routine non-manual workers, skilled manual workers, farmers, etc). The most suitable scheme is that of Erikson and Goldthorpe (15). An easily applicable approximation to this scheme has been developed by Ganzeboon et al. (16) and applied in our international study on inequalities in morbidity and mortality (4).

2. Expressing the socioeconomic status of each occupation by means of their score on one-dimensional scales. Most appropriate are scales that combine information on the average education and average income of people with specific occupations. An international scale of this type has been developed by Ganzeboon et al. (17).

The use of occupation as a socioeconomic indicator is laborious. First, the basic information should be coded according to a 3- or 4-digit classification of occupational titles and, next, a social class scheme or one-dimensional scale should be applied to this occupational classification.

Simple measurement: A much simpler procedure is to ask to the people to assign themselves to a social class. This method has been applied in some international surveys, e.g., the Eurobarometer surveys. The price of this simpler measurement is without doubt a considerable loss of accuracy, but to our knowledge it has never been evaluated to what extent this diminishes the predictive power of measures of social class to health.

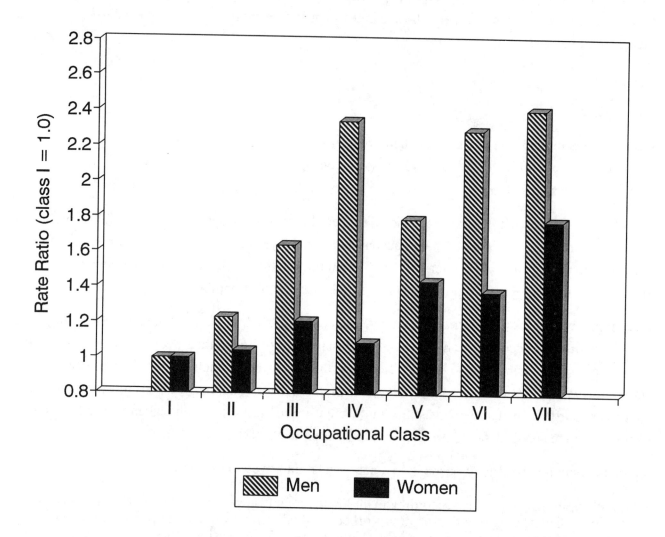

I   = Higher-level employers, managers and professionals

II   = Lower-level employers, managers and professionals

III   = Routine non-manual workers

IV   = Self-employed workers (excluding farmers and professionals)

V   = Technicians, foremen

VI   = Skilled manual workers

VII   = Unskilled manual workers (excluding farm labourers)

Figure 2.   The prevalences of health complaints by occupational class. Eindhoven and surroundings, 1991, men and women 15-74 years. Source: Van de Mheen *et al.* (18)

Example: The use of Erikson-Goldthorpe social class scheme is illustrated in Figure 2. This figure presents the prevalence of health complaints by occupational class in Eindhoven and its surroundings (the Netherlands). The classes of farmers and farm labourers are excluded from Figure 2. Large class variations in health complaints were observed among men and to a lesser extent among women. Men and women in each non-manual class (I to III) report less health complaints than men and women in manual classes (V to VIA). Also men and women in the class of routine non manual workers (III) have relatively low prevalence rates, despite their low income levels and low job status. High prevalence rates are observed among self employed men (IV), but not among women.

THE MEASUREMENT OF SOCIOECONOMIC STATUS AT THE AREA LEVEL

In purely ecological studies, the association between air pollution and health is assessed by comparing the morbidity or mortality rates of urban districts with different levels of air pollution. If the geographic distributions of air pollution and of socioeconomic factors are more or less the same, there is a strong need to control as much as possible for these socioeconomic factors. In this section, we discuss the measurement of area variation in socioeconomicfactors.

We again focus on the measurement of socioeconomic status, but recognise that other potential confounders may work at the area level as well, e.g. the concentration of minority groups in specific areas and environmental degradation of inner city areas. What we would like to stress is that an effective control for the socioeconomic level of areas often requires this factor to be measured separately instead of being mixed up with other factors that operate at the area level.

The socioeconomic status of an area can be measured as some average of the socioeconomic status of each of its residents. This average can be either the arithmetic average of interval variables (educational grade, income level, occupational status score) or the proportion of residents in a specific socioeconomic group.

Education, income and occupation are often closely related at the area level. It is therefore preferable to use composite measures that combine data on education, income and occupation into one socioeconomic index. A simple and effective procedure that has often been applied in British studies is to transform each socioeconomic variable into a variable with a normal distribution (mean 0, standard deviation 1) and then to calculate for each area the sum of its scores on these Z-transformed variables.

Data on both education, income and occupation are often available from population census records. Sometimes, however, data on most of these indicators is lacking and there is a need to use proxy measures in the construction of the composite socioeconomic index. Examples are indicators of material standards of living such as those discussed in section **Income.** Care should be taken that these proxies are, at the area level, valid indicators of the average socioeconomic status of the residents. The careful construction of 'deprivation indices' in British studies is a good example of the ways in which researchers make most out of the limited data that are available (19).

International comparability of proxy measures may be difficult. Indicators that are considered to be reasonably valid in one country may be invalid in other countries. To our knowledge, the unemployment rate of urban districts is the only proxy measure that has proven to be available and valid in cities from different parts of Europe (e.g. 19-21).

Example: Figure 3 illustrates the use of different measures of socioeconomic level in urban areas. In this figure, areas in Barcelona are grouped according to a 'high' or 'low' score on socioeconomic measures. Substantial mortality differences are observed between 'low' and 'high' areas when they are classified according to their income level, educational level or unemployment rate. Much smaller mortality differences were observed when using an indicator of housing conditions, despite the fact that this indicator combined various aspects of housing quality, such as crowding and basic amenities. If, in this case, an epidemiological study would include the housing indicator as the only socioeconomic variable, it would probably fail to adequately control for confounding by socioeconomic factors.

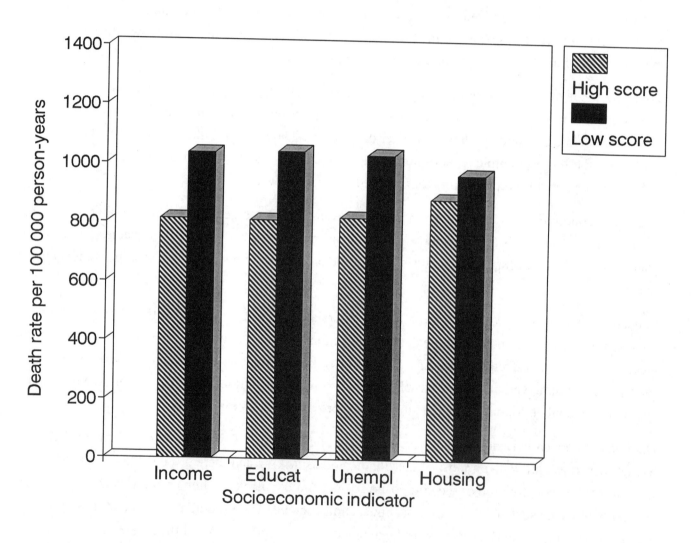

Figure 3. Mortality differences between districts with high and low socioeconomic level, using four different indicators of the socioeconomic level of districts. Barcelona, 1984-1987, all ages and both sexes. Source: Mompart and Pennia (20)

DISCUSSION

Increasingly more efforts are made in air pollution epidemiology to measure accurately the exposure of individual people to air pollution, e.g. with data on time activity patterns. The acquisition of detailed data at the individual level opens up the possibility to make the parallel advances that are so badly needed in the measurement and control for socioeconomic confounders.

Often, a trade-off will have to be made between, on the one hand, the need to control as effectively as possible for socioeconomic confounders and, on the other hand, the wish to keep the measurement of education, income and occupation as simple as possible. Essential to this trade-off is to know in how much detail socioeconomic factors have to be measured to reduce residual confounding to acceptable levels.

Unfortunately, the current knowledge on this issue is far from sufficient. For example, the available literature on socioeconomic inequalities in health provides only fragmentary evidence on the predictive power of different measures of occupation, education or income. Therefore, further work is required both in the fields of both social epidemiology and air pollution epidemiology.

The main contribution of social epidemiology would be:

- to evaluate different socioeconomic measures for their ability to predict health differences related to education, income and occupation respectively;

- to develop a set a simple measures that are able to predict most of the socioeconomic health differences.

The task to air pollution epidemiology would be to evaluate the sensitivity of air pollution effect estimates to different ways of measuring and controlling for education, income and occupation. Experiences in this field should be accumulated for different study designs and for different countries. This accumulation of experience would greatly benefit from attempts to improve the comparability of socioeconomic measures across Europe.

REFERENCES

1. Kunst AE, Mackenbach JP. General overview of the significance of socioeconomic factors on health in Europe. In Jantunen MJ, Viegi G, Nolan C (Eds) *Socioeconomic and Cultural Factors in Air Pollution Epidemiology*. **EC Air Pollution Epidemiology Report Series No: 8,** 1997, 3-12.
2. Kunst AE, Mackenbach JP. The size of mortality differences associated with educational level in nine industrialized countries. *American Journal of Public Health* 1994; **84**; 932-937.
3. Kunst AE, Geurts JJM, van den Berg J. International variation of socioeconomic inequalities in self-reported health. *Journal of Epidemiology and Community Health* 1995, **49**; 117-123.
4. Kunst AE, Cavelaars AEJM, Groenhof F, Mackenbach JP. Country reports to the concerted action "Socioeconomic inequalities in morbidity and mortality in Europe: an international comparison". Erasmus University, Rotterdam, 1994.
5. Kunst AE, Mackenbach JP. Measuring socioeconomic inequalities in health. World Health Organization, Copenhagen, 1994.
6. OECD. Education in OECD countries 1987-89. A compendium of statistical information. 1990 Special Edition. OECD, Paris, 1990.
7. Kunst AE, Cavelaars AEJM, Groenhof F, Geurts JJM, Mackenbach JP, EU Working Group on Socio-economic Inequalities in Health. Socio-economic inequalities in morbidity and mortality in Europe: a comparative study. Erasmus University, Rotterdam, 1996.
8. Mielck A, Rosario Giraldez M (eds.). Inequalities in health and health care. Review of selected publications from 18 Western European Countries. Waxmann, Münster/New York, 1993.

9.   Goldblatt P, Fox J. Household mortality from the OPCS longitudinal study. *Population Trends* 1978; **14**: 20-27.
10. Blaxter M. Health and lifestyles. Routeledge, London, 1990.
11. Martikainen PT. Sociodemographic factors and mortality among Finnish women 1981-85. London School of Economics and Political Science, London, 1993.
12. Martelin T. Mortality by indicators of socioeconomic status among the Finnish elderly. *Social Science & Medicine* 1994; **38**; 1257-1278.
13. Arber S, Ginn J. Gender and inequalities in health in later life. *Social Science & Medicine* 1993; **36**: 33-46.
14. Dahl E. Inequality in health and the class position of women: the Norwegian experience. *Sociology of Health & Illness* 1991; **13**: 492-505.
15. Erikson E, Goldthorpe JH. The constant flux. Clarendon Press, Oxford, 1992.
16. Ganzeboom HBG, Luijkx R, Treiman DJ. Intergenerational class mobility in comparative perspective. *Research in Social Stratification and Mobility* 1989; **8**: 3-84.
17. Ganzeboom HBG, Graaf PM de, Treiman DJ. A standard international socioeconomic index of occupational status. *Social Science Research* 1992; **21**: 1-56.
18. Mheen H van de, Stronks K, Bos J van den, Mackenbach JP. The association between socio-economic status and different health indicators (in Dutch). In: Mackenbach JP (ed.), *Longitudinal study on socio-economic differences in health*. Ministry of Health, Rijswijk (the Netherlands), 1994; 41-57.
19. Morris R, Carstairs V. Which deprivation? A comparison of selected deprivation indices. *Journal of Public Health and Medicine* 1991; **13**: 318-326.
20. Mompart I, Pennia A. An approximation to the social morbidity and mortality in Barcelona. Paper presented to the EAPS Conference "Health, morbidity and mortality by cause of death", Vilnius, 1990.
21. Mackenbach JP, Looman CWN. Living standards and mortality in the European Community. *Journal of Epidemiology and Community Health* 1994; **48**: 140-145.

PSYCHOLOGICAL FACTORS IN AIR POLLUTION EPIDEMIOLOGY

Ree Meertens & Gerard Swaen

Department of Health Education and Department of Epidemiology, University of Limburg
P.O. Box 616, NL-6200 MD Maastricht

SUMMARY

On basis of a review of studies on the psychological effects of air pollution a plea is held for a more multidisciplinary approach to air pollution research. The primary argument is that air pollution may have effects on the psychology as well as on the physiology of human beings. The psychological effects of air pollution may often be of greater importance to human well-being than the biophysical effects: it seems that people often worry far more about air pollution than is defendable from a medical point of view. Moreover, it is argued that, since psychological research reveals more and more results that point to clinically relevant effects of psychological processes on somatic functioning and health related behaviour, air pollution might affect human somatic functioning both by psychological and somatic routes. Although this line of reasoning is still tentative, it seems to be worthy to explore. It is argued that such explorations may identify new confounders in air pollution epidemiology, or could even lead to the conclusion that some confounders that are commonly controlled for, may be better described in some instances as mediating factors between air pollution and health. It is stressed that knowledge about the route by which air pollution affects human health is important when one wants to eliminate or reduce these effects. Finally, possible directions for future research are depicted.

INTRODUCTION

In air pollution epidemiology, socioeconomic and cultural confounders have received attention only recently. Another category of potentially important confounders, namely psychological confounders, seem to have received almost no attention (however, see references 1, 2). However, it is argued here that it may be worthwhile, interesting or necessary to consider the role of psychological factors in future air pollution research.

First an overview is presented of the studies that have been reported in the literature on the effects of air pollution on the psychology of human beings and their behaviour. The overview is not meant as a comprehensive review covering all studies that have been conducted; the idea is to give a concise but representative sketch of the field. Then, the implications of the study results for air pollution epidemiology will be dealt with quite extensively. Finally, conclusions are drawn and possible directions for future research are depicted.

EFFECTS OF AIR POLLUTION ON THE HUMAN PSYCHOLOGY AND BEHAVIOUR

We will discuss the literature on the effects of air pollution on the human psychology and behaviour in four, rather broad categories. Although sometimes these categories are overlapping, and one could think of other classifications, the classification seems adequate for the present purposes. The categories are (a) public attitudes towards air pollution and effects on - mostly outdoor recreative - behaviour, (b) the effects of air pollution on mental health, stress and mood, (c) the effects of air pollution on several measures of violence, and (d) air pollution effects on cognitive functioning and task performance.

Attitudes and behaviour

Numerous studies (mostly surveys) have been undertaken to investigate public attitudes towards air pollution (see reference 3 for an overview). A general conclusion on the basis of the results of these studies is that people indicate that they are annoyed by air pollution and consider it a serious community problem when directly asked. However, whenever they have to rank community problems, air pollution seems to be not very salient in comparison to other community issues (4).

Several studies have found weak effects of the severity of air pollution on frequency of outdoor recreative behaviour. In one study a weak but significant inverse relationship was found between carbon monoxide as well as oxidant levels, and attendance at outdoor recreational sites (5). In another study the number of people participating in 39 recreational activities at 13 different sites were monitored over a two-and-a-half month period in Southern California (6). The sampling period included times during which major fluctuations in photochemical smog and other oxidants occurred. A moderate reduction of (especially outdoor) recreation behaviour under smog conditions was found, also after controlling for likely confounders (e.g. weather conditions).

In exploring the possibility that air pollution affects human health by an indirect psychological route, it would be especially interesting to know whether perceiving air pollution would lead to changes in *health* related behaviour. The experience of living in a polluted area may be expected to have both positive and negative effects on health life styles. For example, on the one hand one might hypothesize that people think it is of no use for them to stop smoking as they live in an air polluted environment. On the other hand, one also might hypothesize that people who perceive their environment as polluted and unhealthy, would react with adopting a life style they perceive as healthy. One might describe the first category of reactions as *self-exempting reactions* (cf 7), the second category as *compensatory reactions*. The effects of self-exempting or compensatory reactions on health however can not be determined without detailed knowledge of the situation and the content of the reaction, as the following example may illustrate. Although one might expect that in general compensatory reactions would affect the individual's health in a positive way, a plausible compensatory reaction to perceived air pollution or malodour would be to keep the windows close. In the case that the air pollution that is perceived in fact is harmless to health, people may expose themselves to a more polluted and unhealthier indoor environment. Thus, in this specific case a compensatory reaction leads to a negative health effect.

To our knowledge, the effects of air pollution on health related behaviour have received little or no attention of researchers. Circumstantially relevant data come from studies that show, for example, that a prevailing belief among smokers is that lung cancer is caused by air pollution (7), or that women with breast cancer or men with laryngeal or pharyngeal malignancies see (air) pollution as one of the major causes of their illness (8, 9). A Danish study (10) found that the majority of a sample of the general population believed that cancer could result from air pollution in the area. Furthermore, respondents (especially respondents with respiratory problems) seemed to be motivated to protect themselves from air pollution, as they reported that they would avoid outdoor activity during a smog episode, and would *not* be willing to avoid car driving (for self-protective reasons). Although such studies suggest that (some) people perceive a strong relation between health and air pollution, it has yet to be shown clearly that perceived air pollution leads to other health relevant behaviours (smoking, alcohol consumption, ventilation of rooms etc.).

Mental health, stress and mood

Laboratory studies as well as field studies have been carried out to assess the effects of air pollution on mental health and mood. In several laboratory studies (11, 12, 13), undergraduates were exposed to odours produced by sulphide and other foul-smelling chemicals. Compared with individuals who had not been exposed, students in polluted settings described their moods and emotions in more negative terms, expressed less liking for individuals not sharing their fate, gave lower evaluations of their surroundings, formed more negative attitudes about social stimuli, and spent less time in a setting. In another study a time-series design was used to unravel the effects of air pollution on various measures of stress and mood (2). Twenty-two female volunteers of a relatively polluted area and a relatively unpolluted area were followed for two months. After control for meteorological conditions analyses revealed area-related effects of SO_2 on mood and stress synchronously as well as with a time-delay of 1 to 4 days. However, pollutants were unrelated to physiological arousal and somatic state. The lack of such associations may be attributed to the small sample, the fact that pollutant concentrations in the polluted area were lower than might have been expected on the basis of previous local annual recordings, and that differences between the polluted area and the non-polluted area were less pronounced than expected. Especially because neuro-endocrine data are known to be subject to large inter- and intra-individual variation, the study may thus have suffered from lack of statistical power.

Although a study of Baum *et al.* (14, see also 15) was not concerned with the effects of air pollution, this study seems to be worth mentioning here, as it shows that the mere *perception* of an environmental threat can lead to changes in a variety of stress levels. Baum *et al.* investigated the medium term effects of the near-accident in the nuclear power station that occurred in 1979 at Three Mile Island (TMI). One year after the near- accident had happened, they compared a group of people living within 5 miles of the damaged reactor with a group of control subjects living 80 or more miles from TMI. Stress measures included self-reports of psychological health and emotional disturbance, measures of concentration and/or motivation for a task, and biochemical estimates of sympathomodularry activity and arousal. Taken together, the data suggest that indeed the TMI area residents were more stressed than the control group. TMI residents exhibited higher levels of both epinephrine and norepinephrine, suggesting heightened sympathetic arousal. Furthermore, TMI area residents perceived greater threats associated with TMI and reported greater symptom distress than did control subjects; they also showed task performance difficulties associated with stress.

Not only moods seem to be affected by air pollution level; at least three studies have shown positive correlations between outdoor pollutants and psychiatric disturbances (16, 17, 18, see also 19, 20). Furthermore, one study (21, cf 22) showed that subjects who perceived poor air quality in their neighbourhood and had experienced a recent, undesirable life event had greater symptoms of depression than subjects who did not perceive poor air quality in their neighbourhood and had experienced a recent undesirable life event. This finding is especially interesting as there is mounting evidence that the combined effects of several stress sources are more severe than one would expect on basis of the effects of these sources alone (23).

Violent acts

As noted before, malodour may lead to lower evaluations of social stimuli, and to less liking of people not sharing the same smelly fate. Such findings have instigated some researchers to examine the effects of air pollution on violent crimes or physical aggression. A field study (23) found that more family disturbances were recorded when ozone levels were high than when they were low (after controlling for confounders like temperature and day of the week). In a laboratory study (13, see also 24) some evidence was found that undergraduate males who were confronted with a moderately unpleasant pollutant were more willing to shock a confederate as a punishment for making errors on a learning task, compared to subjects confronted with an unpolluted environment or with an extremely obnoxious odour. Such an inverse U-curve - with highest aggression levels found with medium levels of the stressor - is often found in stress research; extremely unpleasant stressors are thought to inhibit aggressive behaviour by eliciting incompatible escape responses.

Task performance and cognitive functioning

Numerous experiments have shown impairing effects of carbon monoxide (CO) on human performance (e.g. 25, 26); as the effects however should be attributed to direct somatic effects of carbon monoxide (less oxygen transport to the brain), they are not relevant for the present discussion.

The effects of other pollutants on cognitive functioning and task performance have not received a lot of research attention. In a correlational study, motor vehicle accident frequencies in Los Angeles at particular times of day and days of the week over a period of several weeks, were compared with air pollution data for carbon monoxide and oxidants for those same periods. Non-parametric tests showed significant relationships between oxidant and traffic accidents, but not between carbon monoxide and accidents (27). In the earlier cited study of Bullinger (2) increased pollutant concentrations (especially sulphur dioxide) appeared to be related to impairment in reaction time to visual stimuli and in ability to concentrate.

Rotton (11) exposed subjects to harmless but malodorous pollution (ethyl mercaptan). He found that malodour impaired performance on complex but not simple tasks. When subjects had no control over odour (could not leave the room), they furthermore showed signs of so-called 'aftereffects' (post-stress deficits in performance and frustration tolerance) that are characteristic stressor effects. Rotton concludes that malodorous pollution exerts effects similar to ones produced by noise, density and other stressors.

CONCLUSION AND DISCUSSION

General conclusion

The conclusion from the foregoing overview of the literature on the effects of air pollution on the human psychology and behaviour might be that there seems to be enough evidence that (perception of) air pollution affects the human psychology and human behaviour. We would like to leave this conclusion as general as it is; it is not our purpose to discuss whether or not, for example, there is sufficient evidence for effects of air pollution on aggressive behaviour or on psychiatric admissions. The only conclusion we would like to put forward is that there is sufficient evidence of effects on the human psychology in general to warrant serious attention.

Relevance for air pollution epidemiologists

Our argument here is that the discussed findings may be relevant for air pollution epidemiologists in four different ways (see also Figure 1). First, psychological effects of air pollution have received relatively little research attention; as health is currently defined by the WHO as 'not merely the absence of invalidity or disease' but includes also mental and social well-being, air pollution epidemiologists seem to overlook a possibly important area. Second, psychological factors may interact with the direct effects of air pollution. Third, in some cases air pollution may cause such high levels of stress that this stress may affect somatic functioning (headaches, ulcers, cardiovascular disease, worsening of asthmatic symptoms, impairment of immune function, etc.). Such *indirect* effects via stress on health may in some cases be of the same magnitude as the (often small) *direct* effects of air pollution on human health. The fourth and last point is the most speculative one, as almost no research has addressed this question: the experience of living in a polluted environment may affect health relevant behaviour or life style, which in turn affects health.

Figure 1.   Possible relations between air pollution and health

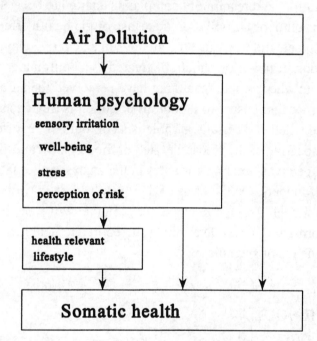

In fact there is a fifth relation between psychological factors and air pollution epidemiology: the concern about air pollution may lead to information bias in exposed people, and to apparent health effects (e.g. more use of health care services, over-report of respiratory symptoms). Indeed research shows that psychological status may partly determine responses to, for example, respiratory symptom questionnaires (28). Furthermore, perception of an environmental threat may lead to changes in medical care habits or diagnostic practices, and thus to changes in incidence data (29). Although epidemiologists generally acknowledge the existence of such biases, they usually just address this problem shortly in the discussion section.

How to handle psychological factors in air pollution research

The total image of psychological, behavioural and somatic effects of air pollution and the interactions between these factors is quite complicated: (a) air pollution may as well lead to psychosomatic symptoms, as well as to somatopsychic symptoms (e.g. effects of CO on cognitive functioning or effects of lead or cadmium air pollution on learning and development; 30, 31); (b) mental and somatic characteristics may determine which kind of behavioural route an individual takes in response upon environmental pollution: self-exemptive or compensatory; (c) special groups, to be identified on psychological characteristics, may be more susceptible to psycho-somatic disease; (4) behavioural reactions may both blur or attenuate direct somatic health effects of air pollution, etc. etc.

Considering this complexity, a goal of future research would be to get a more complete picture of the effects of air pollution first. Air pollution epidemiologists for example could include (a) annoyance questionnaires (e.g. 3), (b) self-reports of health related behaviour, (c) various stress measures like physiological measurements, measures of cognitive functioning and task concentration, self-reports of psychological health and emotional disturbance (e.g. 2, 15), (c) measures of violence or physical aggression (e.g. 24) and (d) mental health measures like psychiatric admissions or depression symptoms (e.g. 17, 18, 19). With increasing empirical knowledge on the various effects of air pollution, the question could shift to the question of which route is responsible for the effects on human health (or, in some cases the absence of effects on human health).

A likely question that will turn up in carrying out such research is 'What is the confounder and what is the effect?'. For example: it might become clear that people keep windows shut because of perceived air pollution, and respiratory complaints aggravate because of exposure to indoor humidity and pollution. If so, is outdoor air pollution the cause of the health effects? In a biomedical sense it is not: outdoor air pollutants did not affect the airways in a negative way. Following this line of reasoning, exposure to indoor air pollution should be treated as a confounder. However, in a certain sense air pollution is the cause: when people would not have perceived the air as polluted, they would have been healthier. In this approach, exposure to indoor air pollution is treated as a mediating variable. In other words, the question as to whether a certain variable is a confounder, an effect or a mediating variable, depends on the perspective of the researcher and or the research question. Of course, researchers may alternate between perspectives, treating variables in the analyses alternately as effects, mediating variables and confounders. On the basis of their results they may discuss what is probably the more 'true' or parsimonious model. Another relevant question that will probably turn up in future research is to what extent information biases determine self-report and health care use data, and what can be done to limit the influence of such biases.

EPILOGUE

Before closing, a relevant issue is whether questions about the route by which air pollution affects health are worth answering. When the effects of pollution are so interwoven and complicated, why not leave this Gordian knot for what it is, and just consider it 'the' health effects of air pollution. Our perspective on this issue is that it is certainly worthwhile to disentangle - and not cut - the knot in this case. Not only because the issue is *theoretically* interesting, but foremost because the issue has *practical* relevance. After all, one would like some action to be undertaken to reduce the effects of air pollution on human health. Of course, the *type* of action one should take depends upon what seems the main route by which air pollution has its effects on health. When negative effects come about by the direct somatic route, governments should set higher standards for the responsible pollutants. However, when adverse health effects come about by indirect mental effects, higher standards are not the solution as long as the public does not perceive the air quality as better; more attention for -for example - risk communication and education about air pollution seems to be a better way here.

Summarizing, the central issue here is that psychological and (health) behavioural effects of air pollution deserve more attention of epidemiologists, as these effects may bring about or interact with somatic consequences of air pollution. Although direct evidence for somatic effects via the indirect mental route is still scarce, and the effects may be expected to be small, more attention for this topic seems to be warranted since the direct effects are often just as small.

REFERENCES

1. Evans GE, Campbell JM. Psychological perspectives on air pollution and health. *Basic and Applied Social Psychology*, 1983, **4**: 137-69.
2. Bullinger M. Psychological effects of air pollution on healthy residents: A time series approach. *Journal of Environmental Psychology*, 1989, **9**: 103-18.
3. Evans GW, Jacobs SV, & Frager NB. Behavioral responses to air pollution. In A. Baum & J. Singer, (Eds.), Advances in environmental psychology. Hillsdale, NJ, Lawrence Erlbaum Associates, 1981.
4. Barker M. Planning for environmental indices. In K. Craik & E. Zube (Eds.), Perceiving environmental quality. New York, Plenum Press, 1976.
5. Chapko MK, Solomon H. Air pollution and recreational behavior. *Journal of Social Psychology*, 1976, **100**: 149-50.
6. Peterson RL. Air pollution and attendance in recreation behavior settings in the Los Angeles Basin, Chicago, IL, American Psychological Association, 1975.
7. Chapman S, Wong WL, Smith W. Self-exempting beliefs about smoking and health: Differences between smokers and ex-smokers. *American Journal of Public Health*, 1993, **83**: 215-9.
8. Ursachenattribution und Krankheitsbewaltigung bei Patientinnen mit Mammakarzinom. *Psychotherapeutische und Psychosomatische Medizinische Psychologie*, 1989, **39**: 232-8.
9. de Maddalena H, Pfrang H. Subjektive Vorstellungen von Laryngektomierten uber die Ursachen ihrer Tumorerkrankung: Zusammenhang mit die psychosozialen Anpassung sowie dem pra- und postoperativen Alkohol- und Tabakkonsum. *HNO*, 1993, **41**, 198-205.
10. Skov T, Cordtz T, Jensen LK, Saugman P, Schmidt K., Theilade P. Modifications of health behaviour in response to air pollution notifications in Copenhagen. *Social Science and Medicine*, 1991, **33**: 621-6.
11. Rotton J. Affective and cognitive consequences of malodorous pollution. *Basic and Applied Social Psychology*, 1983, **4**: 171-91.
12. Rotton J, Barry T, Frey J, Soler E. Air pollution and interpersonal attraction. *Journal of Applied Social Psychology*, 1978, **8**: 57-71.
13. Rotton J, Frey J, Barry T, Milligan M, Fitzpatrick M. The air pollution experience and interpersonal agression. *Journal of Applied Social Psychology*, 1979, **9**: 397-412.
14. Baum A, Fleming R, Singer J. Understanding environmental stress: Strategies for conceptual and methodological integration. In: A. Baum & J. Singer (Eds.), *Advances in environmental psychology*. Hillsdale, NJ, Lawrence Erlbaum Associates, 1985.
15. Foulks E, McLellen T. Psychological sequelae of chronic waste exposure. *Southern Medical Journal*, 1992, **85**: 122-6.
16. Briere J, Downes A, Spensley J. Summer in the city: Urban weather conditions and psychiatric emergency-room visits. *Journal of Abnormal Psychology*, 1983, **92**: 77-80.
17. Strahelivitz N, Strahelivitz A, Miller JE. Air pollution and the admission rate of psychiatric patients. *American Journal of Psychiatry*, 1979, **136**: 206-7.
18. Rotton J, Frey J. Psychological costs of air pollution: Atmospheric conditions, seasonal trends, and psychiatric emergencies. *Population and Environment Behavioral and Social Issues*, 1984, **7**: 3-16.
19. Sorensen LV, Mors O. Social conditions of first-admittance schizophrenics compared with those of the general population. *Nordic Journal of Psychiatry*, 1992, **46**: 367-72.
20. Freeman HL. Psychiatric aspects of environmental stress. *British Journal of Psychiatry*, 1988, **17**: 13-23.
21. Jacobs SV, Evans GW, Catalano R, Dooley D. Air pollution and depressive symptomatology: Exploratory analyses of intervening psychosocial factors. *Population and Environment Behavioral and Social Issues*, 1984, **7**: 260-72.
22. Evans GW, Jacobs SV, Dooley D, Catalano R. The interaction of stressful life events and chronic strains on community mental health. *American Journal of Community Psychology*, 1987, **15**: 23-34.
23. Rotton J, Frey J. Air pollution, weather, and violent crimes: Concomitant time-series analysis of archival data. *Journal of Personality and Social Psychology*, **49**: 1207-20.
24. Jones JW, Bogat GA. Air pollution and human agression. *Psychological Reports*, 1978, **43**: 721-2.
25. Schulte JH. Effects of mild carbon monoxide intoxication. *Archives of Environmental Health*, 1963, **7**: 524-30.
26. Beard RR, Wertheim GA. Behavioral impairment associated with small doses of carbon monoxide. *American Journal of Public Health*, 1967, **57**: 2012-22.
27. Ury HK, Perkins NM, Goldsmith JR. Motor vehicle accidents and vehicular pollution in Los Angeles. *Archives of Environmental Health*, 1972, **25**:314-22.
28. Hatch MC, Wallenstein S, Beyea J, Nieves JW, Susser M. Cancer rates after the Three Mile Island nuclear accident and

proximity of residence to the plant. *American Journal of Public Health*, 1991, **81**: 719-24.
29. Dales RE, Spitzer WO, Schechter MT, Suissa S. The influence of psychological status on respiratory symptom reporting. *American Review of Respiratory Diseases*, 1989, **139**: 1459-63.
30. Stewart-Pinkham SM. Attention deficit disorder: A toxic response to ambient cadmium air pollution. *International Journal of Biosocial and Medical Research*, 1989, **11**: 134-43.
31. Ratcliffe JM. Developmental and behavioural functions in young children with elevated blood lead levels. *Journal of Epidemiology and Community Health,* 1977, **31**: 258-64.

RECOMMENDATIONS

1. SEC factors are not distributed independently of air pollution exposures. Socioeconomical and cultural factors have usually larger health effects than and concern the same diseases and symptoms as air pollution. Therefore SEC factors and air pollution are interdependent variables.

2. SEC factors can strongly affect both exposure and health effect misclassification - but not mortality data.

3. SEC factors have only small effect on individual time series studies, but their effect on comparison and meta-analysis of multiple time series studies is potentially large.

4. SEC factors do not have only an individual, but also a social and cultural component, i.e. they are also group parameters specific for e.g. workplace, housing district, ethnic group, and social group.

5. Not only "objective" but also "subjective" SEC factors are important. People perceive and behave according to both individual and common subjective experience.

6. Of the three socioeconomic determinants, income, education and occupation, income is the most difficult to determine and interpret correctly.

7. The most obvious occupational, economical and educational outliers in a group under investigation should be excluded from the analysis.

8. Socioeconomic and cultural (SEC) factors should be treated not as confounders, but as cofactors or risk factors, and when possible, be included in the model.

9. Different SEC factors should be measured separately, but linked together into an aggregate index, otherwise these - often strongly interdependent - variables could lead to over-control. The most detrimental factors are usually intercorrelated.

10 In case of SEC effect monifiers, every effort should be made to find the causal pathway. In case of SEC interaction a larger sample size and higher resolution in health and exposure measurement is needed. In case of SEC confounding, it should be minimised in study design.

LIST OF PARTICIPANTS

Ursula Ackermann-Liebrich
Dept. of Social and Preventive Medicine
University of Basel
Steinengraben 49
CH-4051 Basel

Laura Carrozzi
CNR Institute of Clinical Physiology
Via Paolo Savi 8
I-56100 Pisa

Luke Clancy
Dublin University
St. James Hospital
Dublin 8

Norbert Englert
Federal Environmental Agency
Institute of Water, Soil and Air Hygiene
Corrensplatz 1
D-14195 Berlin

Matti Jantunen
KTL -Environmental Health
POBox 95
FIN-70701 Kuopio

Ree Meertens
University of Limburg
Department of Health Education & Promotion
POBox 616
NL-6200 MD Maastricht

Suzanne Moffatt
University of Newcastle Upon Tyne
Department of Epidemiology and Public Health
Medical School, Framlington PL
Newcastle Upon Tyne NE2 4HH

Canice Nolan
EC DG XII, D1 SDM 3/50
Rue de la Loi 200
B-1049 Brussels

Klea Katsouyanni
  University of Athens
  Department of Epidemiology
  75 Mikras Asias Str.
  GR-11524 Athens (Goudi)

Ursula Krämer
  Heinrich Heine University
  Medical Institute of Environmental Hygiene
  Auf'm Hennekamp 50
  D-40225 Düsseldorf

Anton E Kunst
  Erasmus University
  Department of Public Health
  POBox 1738
  NL-3000 DR Rotterdam

Peter Lercher
  University of Innsbruck
  Institute of Social Medicine
  Sonnenburgstrasse 16
  A-6020 Innsbruck

Veijo Notkola
  University of Helsinki
  Department of Sociology
  POBox 25
  FIN 00014 University of Helsinki

Peter Phillimore
  University of Newcastle Upon Tyne
  Department of Epidemiology and Public Health
  Medical School, Framlington PL
  Newcastle Upon Tyne NE2 4HH

Ulrich Ranft
  Heinrich Heine University
  Medical Institute of Environmental Hygiene
  Auf'm Hennekamp 50
  D 40225 Düsseldorf

Ivan Skalik
  Regional Institute of Hygiene of Bohemia
  Zelený pruh 95/97
  CZ-14000 Prague 4

Radim Sràm
  Laboratory of Genetic Ecotoxicology
  Pias
  Unichelskeho Lesa 366
  CZ-14000 Prague 4

Giovanni Viegi
  CNR Institute of Clinical Physiology
  Via Paolo Savi 8
  I-56100 Pisa

Bogdan Wojtyniak
  National Institute of Hygiene
  Department of medical Statistics
  Chocimiska 24
  P-00-791 Warsaw

CORDIS

The Community Research and Development Information Service

Your European R&D Information Source

CORDIS represents a central source of information crucial for any organisation - be it industry, small and medium-sized enterprises, research organisations or universities - wishing to participate in the exploitation of research results, participate in EU funded science and technology programmes and/or seek partnerships.

CORDIS makes information available to the public through a collection of databases. The databases cover research programmes and projects from their preparatory stages through to their execution and final publication of results. A daily news service provides up-to-date information on EU research activities including calls for proposals, events, publications and tenders as well as progress and results of research and development programmes. A partner search facility allows users to register their own details on the database as well as search for potential partners. Other databases cover Commission documents, contact information and relevant publications as well as acronyms and abbreviations.

By becoming a user of CORDIS you have the possibility to:

- Identify opportunities to manufacture and market new products

- Identify partnerships for research and development

- Identify major players in research projects

- Review research completed and in progress in areas of your interest

The databases - nine in total - are accessible on-line free of charge. As a user-friendly aid for on-line searching, Watch-CORDIS, a Windows-based interface, is available on request. The databases are also available on a CD-ROM. The current databases are:

News (English, German and French version) - Results -
Partners - Projects - Programmes - Publications -
Acronyms - Comdocuments - Contacts

CORDIS on World Wide Web

The CORDIS service was extended in September 1994 to include the CORDIS World Wide Web (WWW) server on Internet. This service provides information on CORDIS and the CORDIS databases, various software products, which can be downloaded (including the above mentioned Watch-CORDIS) and the possibility of downloading full text documents including the work programmes and information packages for all the research programmes in the Fourth Framework and calls for proposals.

The CORDIS WWW service can be accessed on the Internet using browser software (e.g. Netscape) and the address is: http://www.cordis.lu/

The CORDIS News database can be accessed through the WWW.

Contact details for further Information

If you would like further information on the CORDIS services, publications and products, please contact the CORDIS Help Desk :

CORDIS Customer Service
B.P. 2373
L-1023 Luxembourg

Telephone: +352-401162-240
Fax: +352-401162-248
E-mail: helpdesk@cordis.lu
WWW: http://www.cordis.lu/

European Commission

EUR 17510 — Socioeconomic and cultural factors in air pollution epidemiology — Report number 8

M. Jantunen

Luxembourg: Office for Official Publications of the European Communities

1997 — VI, 117 pp. — 21 x 29.7 cm

ISBN 92-827-9748-1

Price (excluding VAT) in Luxembourg: ECU 13.50